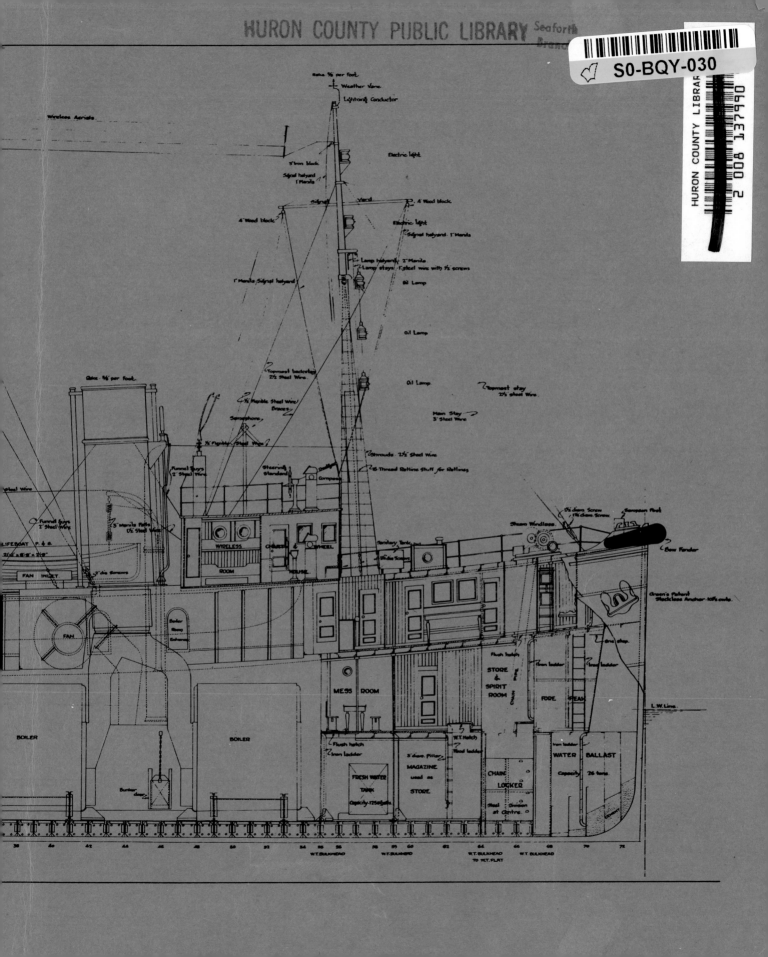

Against Wind and Weather

Against Wind and Weather

The History of Towboating in British Columbia

Ken Drushka

Douglas & McIntyre

Vancouver / Toronto

Douglas & McIntyre Ltd.
1615 Venables Street
Vancouver, British Columbia

Canadian Cataloguing in Publication Data

Drushka, Ken.
    Against wind and weather

    Includes index.
    ISBN 0-88894-327-X

    1. Tugboats. 2. Shipping—British Columbia—
History. I. Title.
VM464.D78   387.2′32′09711   C81-091293-7

Jacket design by Nancy Grout
Typesetting by The Typeworks, Mayne Island
Printed and bound in Canada by D.W. Friesen & Sons Ltd.

To my mother and father

Contents

Preface

When I accepted the proposal to write a history of the towboating industry in British Columbia it sounded fairly simple and straightforward. The subject seemed to have clear boundaries and was not forbidding in its scope, compared to the forest industry, with which I was much more familiar. After all, the towing industry employs only a small fraction of the people who work on the coast of B.C., and the capital investment, compared to the immense sums involved in forestry, is insignificant.

My knowledge of tugs was limited to what I had observed during several years' residence on the sparsely populated coast around Johnstone Strait and Nodales Channel. Tugs were merely one type of vessel that I had to watch out for when I sailed up the coast in a small open boat. I knew that towboats were essential to work and life on the coast. Living and working in logging camps, I had noticed that the large booms of logs, built up over a period of days or weeks, would silently disappear one night. At breakfast the next morning someone would say, "I see the tug came last night." If a logging camp was moved, a tug was involved. If someone ran out of gas or his boat broke down, chances were that a tug helped him out. Gradually, I learned to pick out the distinctive sound of a tug, particularly at night, when the float planes were all grounded and the fish boats were anchored, waiting for daybreak.

The high-pitched scream of a 165-horsepower Jimmy running light past Chatham Point had to be a tug going up the strait for a tow. On the other hand, the low throb, almost below the level of hearing and which I sometimes thought I was imagining, could only be a tug with an Atlas or a Union diesel engine, a fifty-section log boom tied on behind, heading up Nodales Channel to take the inside route through the Yuculta Rapids and on to Howe Sound.

Tugs were always around—even if they could not be seen or heard—day and night, month in, month out. They were a part of the background that people on the coast tend to take for granted, as I did until I started working on this book.

One of the first things that I learned was the complexity of the tugs themselves. At any given time as many as 300 to 400 tugs are working away in the infinity of bays, coves, inlets, channels, sounds and other bodies of water that form the 12,000 miles of B.C. coastline. And every one of these tugs is different. When I talked about tugs to people who know them, I opened a treasure chest of names, builders, owners, engines, captains, crews and stories.

I was warned, and quickly realized, that ten books would not cover the story of all these vessels. Many times I was told: "Go and see such-and-such or so-and-so, he knows everything there is to know about tugs. He's been collecting information for twenty years." When I went to see such-and-such or so-and-so, he would pull out scrapbooks, pictures, files and other bits of information. And invariably he would say: "This is only a small part of it. Go and see . . ."

Early on another factor was brought to my attention when I was discussing the book with Mark Wilson, the marine writer for the Vancouver *Province*. He shook his head and inquired, "How are you going to sort out fact from fiction? None of these towboat people agree on anything. They'll argue for hours about who owned this tug or that. And what kind of engine, and what size, and what finally happened to her.'' He was right.

And so this book in no way claims to be the definitive history of towboating in British Columbia. I have attempted to write a history of the industry that places it in the context of the history of the coast and, I hope, that illustrates the central role it played in the development of this province.

Obviously, I have merely touched on the full story. There is room for half a dozen books on the boats alone. Several, such as the *Lorne,* the *Sea Lion* or the *Sudbury*, might each be worth a book, whereas I could only mention them briefly in passing.

Equally deserving of a far more thorough treatment than they have been given here are the men who worked on the tugs. Men long gone, like George Marchant, captain of just about every tug that sailed these waters during the first decade or two of the industry, or Charles H. Cates, James Warren and James Christensen, who lived the kind of lives that should have become legends.

There are, I know, facets of towboating that I have barely touched upon, yet are, for some people, the essence of the industry. One is the independent owner-operated tug, of which there have been and still are hundreds. Beachcombing, the epitome of towboating for inlanders whose knowledge of the coast is gained from television, is not even mentioned, for it is an industry in itself, bound up with the business of salvaging logs. I point out these omissions not as a convenient means of evading the responsibility I must take for them, but to encourage the writing and publishing of more books on the subject.

Politicians often deplore the fact that Canada, while a maritime nation, does not have a merchant marine, but the fact is that we have a merchant marine which ranks among the best in the world. In large part it consists of the tugs and barges that make up the B.C. towboat fleet, the lifeline that connects the province's economy with that of the world.

During the past few years some of the people involved in the towboat industry, including many whose connections go back to the 1920s and 1930s, became concerned that its story was being lost as the older members of the towboating fraternity passed on.

The Council of Marine Carriers, the association to which most of the larger towboat companies belong, decided to commission a history of the industry and asked me to write it. Initially I was apprehensive because a contract for a commissioned book often contains explicit clauses concerning the right of the sponsors to control the content. The towboat people, it turned out, wanted no such control. Their chief concern was that an honest and independent account be rendered, and I was told to write it as I saw it. With very few exceptions, I have found this to be the attitude of everyone involved in the industry to whom I went for information and assistance. The inadequacies of the book are entirely mine and exist in spite of the best efforts of people in the industry.

Chief among those who helped me is Bill Atwood, chairman of the history committee of the Council of Marine Carriers, who has been involved with towboating for more than forty years. He was able to open doors that I did not know existed. Bill Dolmage, whose encyclopedic knowledge of the industry is legendary, not only provided a wealth of information but also imparted his feeling for towboating, giving me an insight which was invaluable. Ed Reid, Terry Waghorn, Jim Stewart and Russ Cooper all spent long hours patiently answering questions. Capt. Bob MacDonald and the crew of the *Seaspan Cutlass* showed me what the business is like today. Brian Lewis unfailingly came up with precise answers to my vague questions. And scores of other maritime people gave not only their time but also their best wishes. Some of these appear in the aural history sections.

I would also like to acknowledge the assistance given by Len McCann, curator of the Vancouver Maritime Museum, Ron Godden of the Maritime Museum of British Columbia, Derek Reimer of the Provincial Archives of British Columbia, and Jeanette Taylor of the Campbell River Museum.

I have drawn heavily on the three-volume *Marine History of the Pacific Northwest* published by Superior Publishing of Seattle, without which there would be no maritime record of this part of the world. I also owe a great deal to an unpublished manuscript prepared thirty years ago by L.V. Kelly, former marine writer for

the Vancouver *Province*. In a similar way I am indebted
to the unpublished thesis of Donald Beckman on
towboating on the North Arm of the Fraser River, one
of the finest pieces ever written on the industry. Other
valuable resources were *Raincoast Chronicles*, the files
of *Harbour & Shipping* magazine, *Portholes and Pilings*
from the City of Vancouver Archives, and a suitcase full
of scrapbooks generously lent to me by Lloyd Fuerst.

And, finally, I need to thank Brandyn Wilimovsky
who, among other chores, transcribed many, many
hours of tape-recorded interviews.

Against Wind and Weather

1 / The Marine Environment

British Columbia is a huge province with vast
wilderness areas dotted by lakes, high mountain ranges
cut by innumerable rivers, and a long, deeply indented
coastline. The province also has rich natural resources
which have given rise to its principal industries: forest
products, mining and fishing. The development of
these resources resulted in the creation of a number of
small settlements located in a few widely separated
areas. There are few highways or railways, however, as
the long distances between settlements and the rugged
terrain make construction both difficult and
prohibitively expensive. Water transport is, therefore,
the cheapest and most efficient method of moving
bulky raw materials such as logs and coal, heavy
machinery and supplies. Towboats are the workhorses,
the trailer trucks, the freight trains of the coast. They
move the resources that are the wealth of the province
and connect the coastal industries with the world
economy. The development of British Columbia would
not have been possible without the towboat industry,
which is the lifeline of the province.

At any time, hundreds of towboats are chugging
along the coastal waterways, towing log booms, rafts,
barges and scows to processing and transshipment
centres such as the port of Vancouver. They also carry
equipment and supplies to isolated settlements and
work camps up and down the mainland coast, through
the maze of islands and channels in the inside waters,
along the storm-swept west coast of Vancouver Island,
and north to the Queen Charlotte Islands.

A straight line drawn up the coast of the province,
from the 49th to the 60th parallel of latitude, measures

approximately 950 miles. Navigating that same coastline, entering each long inlet and sound, a boat would cover a distance of nearly 12,000 miles. Much of the coast is shadowed by tall mountains, some of it is channelled into dangerous tiderips and rapids, and the rest is open to the rolling breakers of the Pacific Ocean.

Vancouver Island, from its most southerly part near Victoria, runs northwest for 240 miles, ending at Cape Scott. Farther northwest, 100 miles across Queen Charlotte Sound, lies Cape St. James at the bottom end of the Queen Charlotte Islands. These islands run another 150 miles northwest to Langara Point on Dixon Entrance, which separates B.C. from the southern end of the Alaska Panhandle.

Between these two sets of islands and the mainland are the inside waters, sometimes called the inside passage. The outside or western shores of these islands are generally referred to as the west coast.

To the native inhabitants of British Columbia—the Haida, Tsimshian, Kwakiutl, West Coast and Salish peoples—this area was a paradise. Their chief food, the salmon, was abundant. The climate was mild. And the beaches were lined with giant cedar trees, 10 to 12 feet in diameter, which could be carved into graceful dugout canoes. Their craft were ideally suited to these waters, since they could be sailed in front of the wind or paddled up and down the channels. They also drew very little water and could safely navigate areas of tidal

1. The *Westminster Tyee* (Westminster Tug Boats), a 40-foot, 680-horsepower general-purpose tug, pulling a railcar barge on the Fraser River.

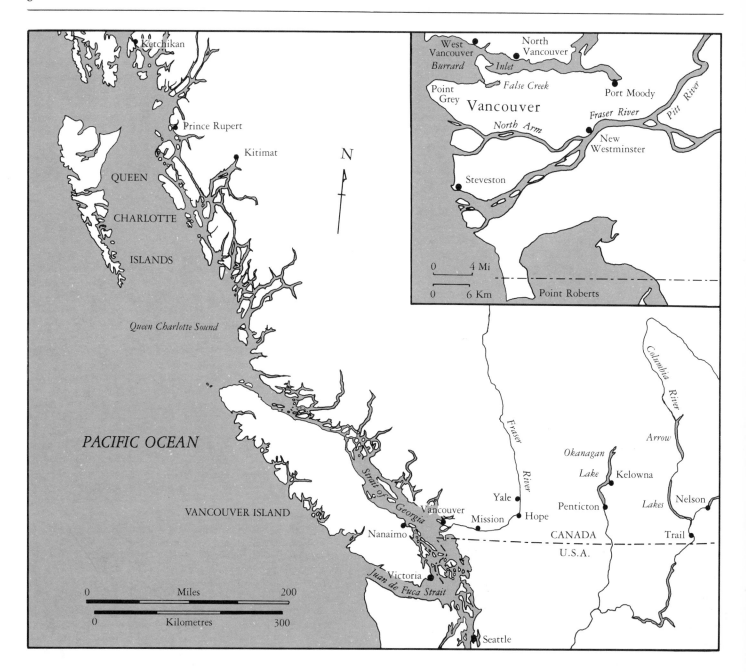

The coast of British Columbia

2. The *Georgia Straits* (Straits Towing) with a
loaded chip barge in tow in the early 1960s.

turbulence. A large canoe could hold two to three tons of freight or perhaps fifty people—and if most of them were paddling, it could move at a speed of 12 to 15 knots.

During the eighteenth and nineteenth centuries, Spanish and English explorers and traders began to occupy the area, drawn by the rich natural resources of fur, timber and fish. Their sailing ships were admirably suited to the task of crossing the wide oceans of the world but they needed a lot of room in which to manoeuvre, so were quite likely to meet with disaster when entering the confines of a strait or channel. Consequently, the first European settlements were on the west coast of Vancouver Island, and the first timber exports were made from Nootka Sound on the island in 1788. Early mariners had no reason to enter Juan de Fuca Strait until George Vancouver went up it and charted the inside waters, confirming that Vancouver Island was, in fact, an island.

The challenge to early mariners of navigating the entrance of Juan de Fuca Strait was increased by the tide, wind, current and weather conditions. The tide approaches the west coast from the southwest. In the open Pacific, it is only about 1.5 feet in height, but climbs as it encounters the shoreline and the entrances to the inside waters. At Cape Flattery, the entrance to Juan de Fuca Strait, the enormous tidal turbulence extends for miles into the Pacific. The violence of these waters can be heightened by a northwest wind, which pushes against the main current. Some of the wild tiderips and overfalls are capable of capsizing a 100-foot boat. The wind also creates enormous swells that can drive ships upon the sloping beaches of the western shores, where they will be pounded to pieces in the heavy surf. These swells give the west coast its own particular character.

Fog can settle in at any time in this area, particularly in the summer and early fall. During the rest of the year, visibility may be obscured by rain or snow. This restricted visibility, coupled with deep inshore waters which make soundings impossible, meant that early mariners in this part of the world often did not have the vaguest idea where they were. Yet they had to accurately estimate when they had cleared Cape Flattery, the northernmost point of the Washington shore, then change course to the southeast

and, hopefully, sail up the middle of the strait. If they were wrong, out of the fog, rain or snow would appear the crashing surf of the Vancouver Island shore. In all likelihood they would not have the space or time to manoeuvre and would be driven ashore somewhere between Port Renfrew and Nootka Sound. Since 1800 about 250 ships have met this fate, earning for this stretch of B.C. coastline the name ''Graveyard of the Pacific.''

The dangers facing sailing masters when they tried to enter Juan de Fuca Strait were once described by Charles Warren Cates. He was a son of Charles H. Cates, an early towboat captain who founded C.H. Cates & Sons Ltd., a towing company that is still

active today. Charles W. was also a towboat captain, and one of the most articulate and knowledgeable experts on the weather and tidal conditions of coastal British Columbia.

As you know, the Straits of Juan de Fuca [Juan de Fuca Strait] lie[s] southeast and northwest, more or less, and the old captains told me when I was a boy that when the prevailing wind is coming in on the estuary of the Columbia, it will come up south of the Olympic Peninsula in through by Olympia, up Puget Sound and out the Straits of Juan de Fuca to meet the parent wind at the entrance of the Strait.

That was a terrible condition because square riggers like Cape Horners or those ocean travellers which were square rigged on all masts were very poor handlers, and they wouldn't tack up into the wind very high, only about 22° above the right angle. They would come in especially if they were strangers, with every hope of making the Straits of Juan de Fuca with a fair wind, and suddenly would be taken aback by a wind coming out of the Straits of Juan de Fuca. They would be taken aback, go northward more or less out of control and go ashore along the Canadian shore all the way up to Nootka Sound.

Most of the wrecks were between Carmanah [Point] and Barclay [Barkley] Sound. There were many terrible wrecks. The Janet Cowan was one that got taken aback in such a manner that she sailed stern first into the beach, smashed and sank. Her crew got away but on shore that winter, there was quite deep snow on the ground and they did not know whether they were on the coast of Washington or the coast of B.C.

3. The *La Garde* (Vancouver Tug Boat) towing in tandem two barges loaded with logs, from Bella Coola to Vancouver, 1959. The 85-foot tug was built in 1942 and had the 300-horsepower Washington diesel out of the first *La Reine*.

The crew split up in two parties, one party went north along the coast and one party went south. The party that went north eventually came to Barclay Sound and the Alberni Canal and got help. When they came back, one of the men of the rescue party, who was a friend of mine, told me they found seven of the crew all huddled together on a log and when they touched them, they all fell over—they were frozen stiff. The sad part was that the stern of the Janet Cowan went so high into the bush that if they had just stayed with the ship they could have lived, as there was food, etc., but they just got panic-stricken.

I am telling you this story to show what the coast was like in the early days. There is one place on the coast where there are the remains of three ships one on top of the other.

The essential character of the British Columbia coast, however, is to be found in the inside waters—the long, convoluted coastline which is protected from the direct influence of the open Pacific. Most of this area lies east of Vancouver Island and the Queen Charlotte Islands. The fury and the power of the open ocean are broken on their western coasts. To the east lies an area unlike any other in the world. It is an intricate maze of islands, channels, inlets, sounds, straits and gulfs—just about every imaginable geographic feature associated with the meeting of ocean and land.

There are three main entrances to the inside waters: Juan de Fuca Strait; Queen Charlotte Sound (entered when travelling south around the top end of Vancouver Island) or Hecate Strait (when going north around the bottom end of the Charlottes); and Dixon Entrance, the 30-mile-wide route which runs due east towards Prince Rupert.

The chief factor to take into account in navigating the inside waters is the tide. It flows through some channels at a sedate 2 or 3 knots and through others in a boiling, seething rush of 20 knots, creating massive overfalls, whirlpools and back eddies.

Starting in the south, the tide pours through the 10-mile-wide, 60-mile-long Juan de Fuca Strait, rising and falling twice each day, never at the same time. The water in the strait constantly reverses direction as the tides go in and out. The strait ends at Victoria. Extending south for 100 miles into the state of Washington lies Puget Sound. To the north is Haro Strait, which leads into the Gulf Islands and the Strait of Georgia. The narrow passages among the Gulf Islands create tidal currents of up to 8 knots in some

4. The sailing ship *Pamir* in a gale off Cape Flattery in 1946.

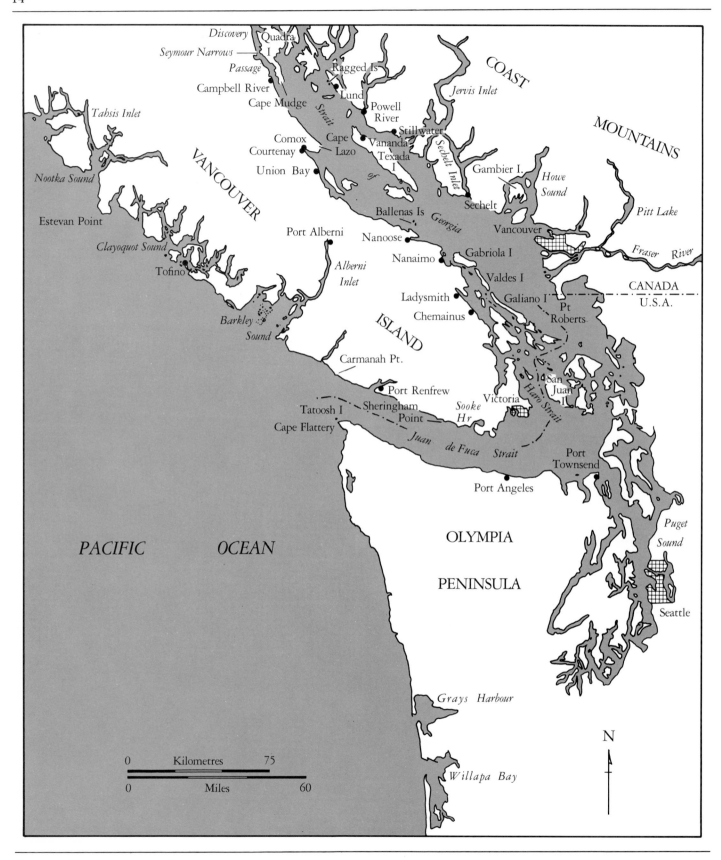

Vancouver Island, southern portion

places. The crest of the tide takes about six hours to move through the islands. Then, in another thirty minutes, the tide traverses the 130-mile length of the Strait of Georgia and is moving up the deep inlets in the mainland: Burrard, Jervis and Toba.

The mainland has twelve major inlet systems, with another four on Vancouver Island and one, Masset Inlet, in the Charlottes. Very little is the same about any two inlets, except that each has a mouth where the tide runs in and out and most of them have one or more major river systems emptying into their upper reaches. Each inlet presents a different set of hazards and challenges to a mariner.

Knight Inlet reaches almost 70 miles into the Coast Mountains. Its sheer rock walls end more than 6,000 feet up in the mountain peaks. There are few places to anchor or find cover, but the tides are fairly consistent and offer no particular hazard to navigation.

Sechelt and Seymour inlets, however, have bottleneck entrances through which the tide boils with great speed and violence. The entrance to Seymour Inlet, Nakwakto Narrows, is only 1,000 feet wide. Every day the tide flows in twice and out twice in an attempt to alternately fill and drain a network of four connecting inlets having a shoreline of 700 miles. The tidal currents here often reach a speed of 24 knots, perhaps the swiftest tidal rapids in the world, and slack water is only a few minutes in duration. Charles W. Cates passed on this account of what occurs at Nakwakto Narrows.

A friend of mine once told me that during a heavy storm he set up a surveyor's transit on the shore and measured the huge tidal swells that formed with the outgoing torrent of water.

He said that there were three huge waves standing stationary which were seventy feet from base to crest. Even the whales know the danger of these rapids and stay in the bays and wait for slack water.

Inlets also present a special danger during certain kinds of winter weather. Many of the mainland inlets reach far back into the interior and, therefore, are subject to interior weather conditions. When a winter high pressure area is centred over the northern interior, the heavy, cold air spills into the heads of the inlets through the river valleys and roars down the

inlets at velocities of up to 100 miles an hour. Any ship attempting to cross the mouth of one of these inlets encounters both extremely rough water and freezing temperatures. This combination can cover a ship in ice and sink it very quickly, unless the crew can find some place protected from the wind and spray to chop off the ice. The situation is as dangerous for a modern tug as it was for a nineteenth-century sailing ship.

At the top end of the Strait of Georgia, near Quadra Island, the Juan de Fuca water meets the tide coming in from the northern entrances to the inside passage. The northern tide runs down Queen Charlotte Strait, filling Blackfish Sound and Kingcome and Knight inlets. Then it rushes down the two-mile-wide

Alex Rodgers
Retired towboat captain

The wind comes up fast down around Victoria here, and southwest winds can pick up real fast. We took a scow into Sooke one day and we were going back into Port Renfrew. I think it was on the *Sirmac*. It was maybe a five-mile-an-hour wind and there was just barely a ripple when we came back out on our way to Port Renfrew. When we got off Sheringham Point, it was blowing seventy-five miles an hour. That's how fast it came up, in less than an hour.

We kept heading up slowly, trying to turn back because everything's just coming right over us, even though we're running slow. Just when we turned back, it eased off. Lasted, I would say, about two or three hours and then it eased off a bit.

Another time we came out of Beecher Bay and weren't even as far as Sooke when we saw this big white cloud coming. It looked just like a fog coming in. Next thing I know it was just off the boat and what it was was water spouts. I figured it came up to about eighty, just bang like that. We called the fellows in the bay to tell them so they could stand by the barges. It lifted the logs that the barges were tied to right out of the water.

You start out thinking it's a beautiful day, and then the wind comes up fast. Sometimes you don't even get a forecast on it.

5. The steam tug *Mighty Mite* (Mite Towing) breaking ice near Marpole Bridge on the Fraser River, 1924. She sank off Bowen Island in 1925 after hitting a deadhead in the late evening.

Johnstone Strait until it reaches the constriction created by Sonora and Quadra islands, which are squeezed between Vancouver Island and the mainland near Bute Inlet.

This area has some of the most hazardous and awe-inspiring features of the inside passage. There are two main channels through the maze of islands and fast-flowing water. The first, at the mouth of Bute Inlet, is through a twisting passage called Yuculta Rapids. The Yucultas comprise two sets of rapids, those between the Dent Islands to the north and those between the Gillard Islands at the south end. Navigating the Gillard Rapids, when heading north, requires a hard left turn between the islands. Getting through the Dents

involves either making a 90-degree turn and going up Tugboat Pass between the islands, or going straight into the rapids along the Sonora Island shore. Because of the restricted width of the channels here—Tugboat Pass is only 700 feet wide—currents of 10 knots are common. There are huge tiderips and whirlpools.

Charles W. Cates tells the following tale about his pioneering father's first encounter with the Yucultas:

My father told me that when he first came to the coast he decided to go prospecting. He and "Navvy Jack" Thomas . . . bought a large rowboat from Andy Linton, and started up the coast. There were no tide books in those days, and I presume father and "Navvy Jack" didn't have charts. One evening they camped on a little island in a narrow

6. The *Pacific Monarch* (Pacific Coyle Navigation)
all iced up, docked at Anyox in February 1927.

channel. Father said that in the middle of the night "Navvy Jack" woke him up. In great excitement he said the island had come alive and was steaming away with them. Father said it was quite eerie to see the island with a huge bow wave on it. Of course it was just that they were on upper Dent Island, during a big tide.

Owing to the crooked channel there is an entirely different action than to the Seymours. The tide swirls and boils in all directions, in some parts forming huge whirlpools, which locally are called "The devils dishpans." These are big enough to suck down a launch and have a very weird feeling when they grip a small boat, even when the tide is nearing slack water.

The second channel through this maze of islands, Seymour Narrows, lies between Quadra and Vancouver islands, at the south end of Discovery Passage. Charles W. Cates also describes the awesome force of these rapids:

Let me try to describe to you the wonderful sight of the Seymours in full force. It is possible to get into Menzies Bay on the Vancouver Island shore with a small boat, work out behind the point near Ripple Rock and watch the tide pour in on its way southward to the Gulf [Strait] of Georgia. The channel is one-third of a mile wide with Ripple Rock one hundred yards across, fourteen feet below the surface. As the tide sweeps in it fairly shakes the surrounding shores. Huge eddies wheel and boil, with flocks of seagulls, ducks and eagles, flying around watching for fish that have been injured in this terrific upheaval of nature. The water seems to flicker as it tears in through this narrow passage. Every few

6

Lloyd Sias

Former towboat captain;
master, Port McNeil-Alert Bay ferry

Johnny Campbell was a real good skipper and I had some experiences with him that were quite the experiences. One of them I'll never forget. That winter we were on the *Sea Queen*, packing herring for Canadian Fish. This was a towboat, but we were packing herring. The *Sea Queen* had a hatch forward.

We had an awful big load of herring. We were coming down, I think, from the Namu area. We got down off Cape Lazo and it was blowing northerly, Squamish winds out of the inlets—freezing. We were icing up bad and a line broke. We had twin booms on her, and the hook on the running line broke loose, so every time we dove into a sea the doggone thing headed for the window. It came just about a half inch from the wheelhouse window.

Not a thing we could do about it out there. I'll tell you, that was a harrowing experience. We finally got in under Ballenas Island, got it secured and chopped some ice off.

When we got into Steveston and went to the Canadian Fish plant, we had such a load of ice on that they couldn't believe the ship was still floating. I still think that the reason we made it into Steveston was from Johnny's superb seamanship.

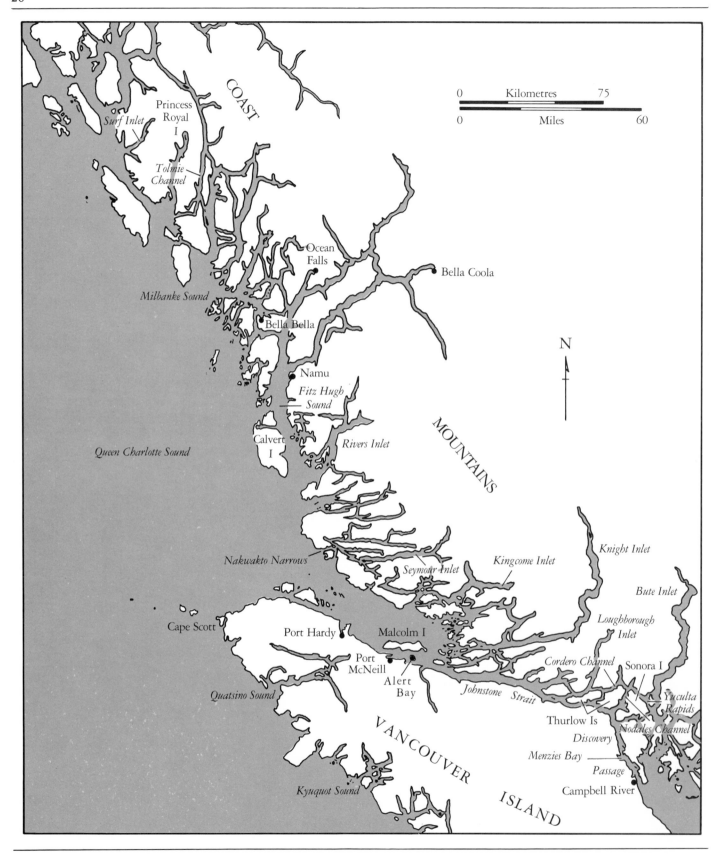

Vancouver Island, northern portion

seconds the stream will erupt like a depth charge, and raise a mushroom of water, as big as a city lot, fully two feet above the surrounding surface. This only lasts a few seconds and the surface is quite smooth again. The tide rushes on to Race Point a mile away, where it piles up in white foam. The current there is deflected, some swirling in to Menzies Bay on the right hand shore, the rest rushing swiftly up past Campbell River and Quathiaska Cove, to finally reach the Gulf of Georgia at Cape Mudge, seven miles south of the narrows.

When a south-east gale is blowing the tide rips in this area are some of the worst on the coast. These rips are extremely treacherous as it is in this area that the north and south tidal streams collide causing not only extremely heavy seas in stormy weather but they also cause great masses of drifting logs and other flotsam to collect thus creating a severe hazard for any vessel running at night in this locality.

In 1958, after a number of unsuccessful attempts to drill blasting holes into Ripple Rock from an anchored barge, a shaft was sunk in Maude Island on the east side of Seymour Narrows. It was extended under the narrows and up into Ripple Rock, where a large cavern was blasted out. Into this was packed 1,375 tons of dynamite. The explosion that followed took 37 feet off the twin peaks of the obstacle. Although this did not slow down the current appreciably, it diminished the turbulence and removed a major hazard from the middle of the channel. By that time, the rock had claimed about a hundred lives.

The tides along the northern part of the B.C. coast behave differently from those in the inside passage, since there is no large, enclosed body of water like the Strait of Georgia to be filled via narrow passages. The major tidal feature is the wide range of rise and fall. This is largely the result of the configuration of Hecate Strait, which lies between the Queen Charlotte Islands and the islands that hug the mainland. At its northern end, near Prince Rupert, the strait is 40 miles wide and only 10 fathoms deep; the tidal range is 26 feet. At its southern end, near Bella Bella, the strait is 80 miles wide and 200 fathoms deep; the tidal range is 15 feet.

The northern mainland coast is composed of chains of islands and long, narrow passages like Grenville Channel between Pitt Island and the mainland. Most channels fill up gradually from each end, with the tides meeting in the middle. The only real stretch of the inside passage that is open to the Pacific is the 35 miles

Mickey Balatti
Retired towboat captain

We got caught in that big rip off Cape Mudge one time, when I was mate on the *Pacific Monarch* with old Dick Jones. We were taking a barge north to Queen Charlotte Islands. I came off watch at Cape Lazo and told old Dick, "We're going to hit the tide wrong at Cape Mudge. You want to slow down?"

"Oh, no," he said, "this has crossed the ocean three times. We won't stop for anything."

Well, I went to bed and I knew she was going to be tough. Then the deck hand came down to call me. "Hurry up! Shorten up, shorten up!" he says. "We're turning around. We're in the tiderip."

So I jumped out of my bunk and ran aft. The steam winch was always on steam, and the exhaust was always on condense—on vacuum—so you could open up that winch and run her any time. You didn't have to put the draincocks on because she was always drained. I ran down, took the brake off, opened the throttle and started heaving. We were making a big circle. Well, you've got to heave in your towline fast or that big bight will drop on bottom and hook up.

We were just on the edge of the tiderip, and that rip would boil up and then she'd flatten down. There was a ladder from the winch up to the top deck. We hit another tiderip and she just boiled over the stern of that tug, and the tug was under about six feet of water. It was all broken water, she wasn't solid water. I ran up that ladder and in about three or four minutes it flattened down again, so I ran down again and stood by the winch, which was still going all this time. Three times I was chased away from that winch before we got out of it.

Old Dick Jones was pretty bloody scared when I got up in the wheelhouse. He didn't think it would be that bad, but that was like a lot of things with boat men. Lots of times you might be lucky and come through something. Then you've got a second chance—but sometimes you only have one chance.

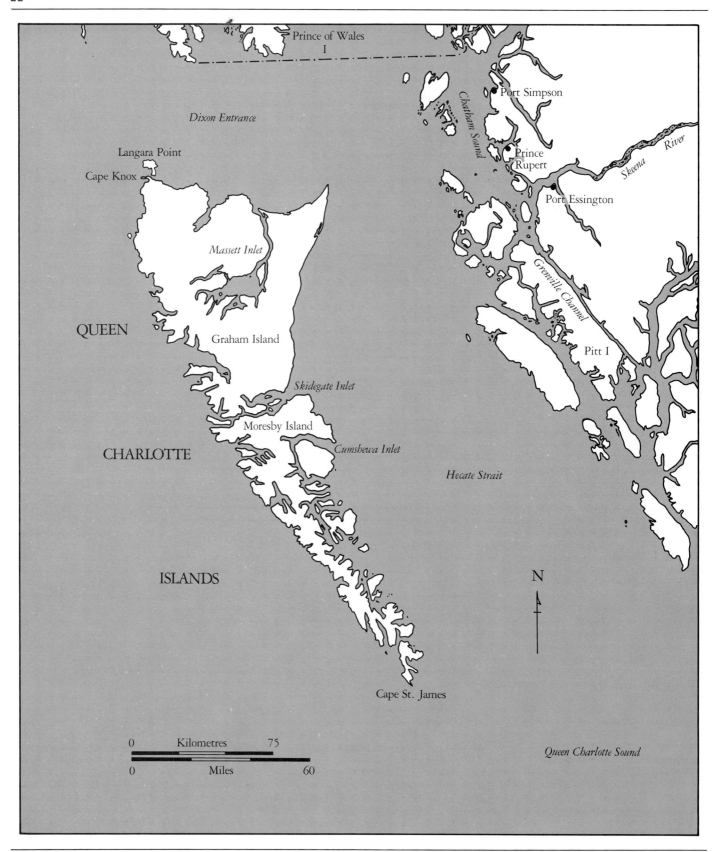

Queen Charlotte Islands and north coast

extending south from Calvert Island to the northern tip of Vancouver Island.

Generally, however, the coastal waters of British Columbia are not hazardous. Most of the time, they are places of spectacular beauty. And though the open west coast may be a formidable and even terrifying place in a gale, it is an altogether different experience to be out there in a light sea, under clear skies, rolling easily with the swells. The inside passage, too, has many pleasures. A long, slow tow down Johnstone Strait, fishing lines out and the scenery sliding past, more than compensates for the occasional harrowing trip. The narrow, winding channels north of the Seymours and the Yucultas—that rugged and sparsely inhabited area that towboaters call the ''jungle country''—are filled with wildlife, marine life and the various activities and enterprises of loggers, fishermen and beachcombers. Because the channels are narrow, everything is close at hand. This part of the coast has an appealing intimacy.

The hazards and the dangers, because dramatic, are simpler to describe. But the people who work on tugs know the contentment of bringing a tow down Queen Charlotte and Johnstone straits, catching the last of the flood tide at the Seymours just before dark, then making the long haul across the placid Strait of Georgia, while watching the glow of Vancouver rise in the southeastern sky. Headed home.

Ed Taylor
Retired towboat captain and dispatcher

The early skippers that I sailed under, they'd never run Seymour Narrows. Never! They'd come down and wait for the last hour so they could get round and get past Cape Mudge before the ebb starts. The same way going northbound; they'd never run it.

Then I got going with a skipper—boy! I learned more from him by his mistakes than I would learn from a guy who really knew what he was doing. I was mate with him on a big tug we had then called the *La Pointe* and it had eight hundred horsepower. It's still going too, by the way. Anyway, it's midnight and we're right off Campbell River. It was a beautiful moonlit night, a big moon like a dollar. And this captain used to let out every bit of towline at Prospect Point—now, there'd be about twelve hundred feet of line out—and he used to heave it up when he got to Ocean Falls. Full out, and here's Seymour.

The skipper says, ''Well, she's all yours. You've got a fair tide.''

I says, ''We certainly have. Look, I'm going to take in about a thousand feet of towline.''

He says, ''What for? We're not going to waste time taking in towline. Goodnight.''

So away we go. And I'd never run that hole in my life. Training under the old-timers, it was pretty near slack when we went through—but not this time. It's just a-boiling, you can see it from Race Point. You can see the hole, and it's white, just white water. Well, boy, I'm starting to count my beads, I'll tell you. We're heading in there with all that line out, and I'm praying to God that there's nobody going to be bucking south—boats like the *Prince Rupert* or the *Prince George*, they could buck a sixteen-knot tide.

Well. We hit the hole. At one time on this big tug they used an old steam engine and converted it to air for steering, so you had to pull it. You couldn't spin the wheel, not like an ordinary geared engine. And here's these swirls and the big holes—it was just like hell in there. And the boat's swinging like mad.

After we got by the rock, I just left it amidship and she went through herself. But boy, was it ever a thriller. And now everybody does it.

7. The *Jean L* (Lyttle Bros.) running light off Point Atkinson lighthouse at the entrance to Burrard Inlet circa 1956.

2 / Days of Sail and Steam

During the first few decades of the nineteenth century, the dominant economic influence in northern North America was the Hudson's Bay Company. In 1821 the company secured from the British government exclusive trading rights for a vast area north of the 49th parallel, between the Great Lakes and the Rocky Mountains. On the Pacific coast, the company's territory stretched from the Columbia River to the Alaska Panhandle, including the lands in the interior that now comprise British Columbia.

In 1825 the Hudson's Bay Company established its headquarters at Fort Vancouver on the Columbia River and a year later George Simpson, a dynamic and perceptive figure, was appointed governor-in-chief in North America. Ranking high among the many problems confronting Simpson were competition from independent American traders, and the difficulties encountered by the company's sailing ships in navigating the coastal waters of the Pacific northwest. These ships came from England with trade goods, supplies and company employees. They took on a load of furs, fish and timbers and carried on across the Pacific to China. There, they did more trading, took on tea, silk and spices and returned to England. The loss of a number of ships on the Columbia River bar prompted Simpson to submit a proposal to his superiors:

The advantages which a Steam Vessel would possess over sailing craft in navigating the rivers, inlets and sounds, which are so numerous on that coast, and where all the trade is made, embolden us to request that Your Honors will be pleased to provide a Vessel of that description. We are aware that the first cost would be heavy, but we feel assured that she would, in a very short time, become the cheapest craft that could be used, and perform more effective service than any two Sailing Vessels which might be provided. . . .

A Steam Vessel would afford us incalculable advantages over the Americans, as we could look into every Creek and cove while they were confined to harbour by head winds and calms, we could ascend every stream of any consequence upon the coast, we could visit our establishments at stated periods, in short a Steam Vessel would, in our opinion, bring the contest to a close very soon, by making us masters of the trade.

In 1836, Simpson eventually got his steamboat—the first on the Pacific coast. The *Beaver*, rated at 109 tons, was just over 100 feet long, with a beam of 20 feet and a draft of 8.5 feet. The two engines of 35 nominal horsepower drove paddle wheels mounted on each side. The vertical cylinders had a bore of 42 inches and a 36-inch stroke. The boilers burned wood or coal, and her large crew often included thirteen woodcutters. The working pressure was so low that the ship was unable to blow her whistle while in motion.

The *Beaver* was intended to be a freighter, moving cargo up and down the coast. However, the boat's owners very quickly found a more important task for her to perform, as indicated by the log entry for her first day of operation, 17 May 1836:

At daylight unmoored ship and got the steam up. At 3:30 weighed and ran down abreast of the lower plain for firewood. At noon lashed alongside the Columbia. At 1:30

took the Columbia in tow up to the saw-mill. At 6 returned and anchored off Fort Vancouver in 5 fathoms.

From the very beginning the *Beaver* worked as a towboat. Of course, she was put to many other uses—freighting, carrying passengers, charting and surveying—but at the start and for the last years of the boat's life her primary function was to assist in moving other craft or logs through the complicated waters of the north Pacific coast.

In the late 1840s, two of the province's main industries had their beginnings: lumber and coal. In 1847, the first shipment of spars was sent to England, and the next year the Hudson's Bay Company built a sawmill in Victoria to supply the local market. The lumber industry was slow to develop and for many years was limited to the Victoria mill, a second Hudson's Bay Company mill in Sooke and a small family-run mill in Sooke.

In 1849, coal mining began at Fort Rupert on the northern end of Vancouver Island. The immediate market for the coal was to provide fuel for steamers on the Pacific Mail Steamship Company's recently inaugurated run between Panama and Oregon. The incentive was the price of coal, which had reached forty dollars a ton in San Francisco.

As it turned out, there was very little coal at Fort Rupert and it was of poor quality. But by then the precious substance had been found at Nanaimo, of a quality and in quantities deemed adequate to supply the merchant steamer fleets of the Pacific. The first shipment went to San Francisco on the *Recovery* in 1852. Robert Dunsmuir was the manager of these mines. Within thirty years, he had negotiated a deal with the federal and provincial governments which gave him a cash subsidy of $750,000 and 1.9 million acres of Vancouver Island timberlands and coalfields. In exchange he built the seventy-nine-mile-long Esquimalt and Nanaimo Railway.

As coalfields were opened up from Nanaimo to Comox, sailing ships came from all over the Pacific to haul coal for industry, as well as to provide fuel for the growing steamship operations which were beginning to replace sail. The task of getting these sailing ships into harbour from the open seas off Cape Flattery and out to sea again once they were loaded called for large,

powerful tugs. And the same commodity, coal, provided the fuel for the tugs, replacing the bulkier, less convenient wood.

In the 1850s, the small amount of ship towing up and down Juan de Fuca Strait was done by American boats out of Puget Sound, such as the *Resolute* and the *Ranger No. 2*. The *Beaver* towed the odd ship, as did a second Hudson's Bay Company steamer, the *Otter*.

As the traffic in shipping increased, harbours were improved and loading facilities were constructed. In Nanaimo, the Hudson's Bay Company built the first wharf from which to load coal ships bound for California. Soon, 33,000 tons a year were being exported. Victoria, through which most of the prospectors and equipment passed en route to the Fraser River in the gold rush of 1857, was beginning to resemble San Francisco harbour.

With the arrival of about 5,000 gold seekers on the Fraser, the local demand for lumber mushroomed. Mills were built at Yale and Harrison Lake. When the Cariboo gold rush started in 1860, more mills were built on the future site of New Westminster, and Pioneer Mills was built on Burrard Inlet.

The first major milling operation for export began on Vancouver Island. It was organized by Edward Stamp, an English sea captain who had come to Puget Sound for a load of spars in 1855 and returned to build a mill at the head of Alberni Canal. Anderson's Mill, as it was called, began cutting in 1861 and made lumber shipments to Peru, Australia and Hawaii. The following year, fourteen ships loaded out of Alberni with more than eight million board feet of lumber. These ships were towed in and out of the canal by what many people regard as the island's first tugs, the *Thames* and the *Diana*. Neither, however, had been designed for that purpose. The *Thames* had been built to haul livestock between London and Hamburg; the *Diana* had come from China to serve as a launch for the Pacific Mail Company. In 1865, Edward Stamp and Thomas Pamphlet (another English sea captain, who had been a master of the *Beaver*) organized a second large mill, this time in Burrard Inlet. Stamp obtained timber leases stretching from Burrard Inlet to the Fraser River. Being as short on business sense as he was long on vision, Stamp was forced to pull out within a short time. The mill was later bought out by English interests and reorganized as the Hastings Sawmill Company in 1870.

Meanwhile, on the north shore of the inlet, Sewell Prescott Moody bought Pioneer Mills, which had been built a few years earlier. He expanded this operation enormously and obtained timber leases on much of the north shore. Eventually it became the Moodyville Sawmill Company. In 1877, the DeBeck brothers started the Brunette Sawmill Company on the Fraser River. The lumber industry was off to a good start in B.C.

In those days logs were brought directly from the stump to the mill by oxen or horses along skid roads. When Jeremiah Rogers began logging for Stamp in Kitsilano, some of his logs were moved across English Bay, through the First Narrows and up to the mill with the aid of rowboats and kedge anchors. At that time, sawmills used tugs only to tow ships from the open sea off Cape Flattery into the harbours and back out again, not to tow logs.

Stamp spent $50,000 having the province's first tugboat built in Victoria, the *Isabel*. Thomas Pamphlet was her first captain. In 1866 she started towing ships to and from the Stamp and Moody mills to the open sea, starting with five ships in 1866 and rising to forty-five by 1869 as the export lumber business became better established.

The McAllister brothers of Victoria built a giant of

8. The Hudson's Bay Company's *Beaver*, the first steam-powered boat on the North Pacific coast, photographed in Victoria harbour, 1870.

a tug, the 180-foot side-wheeler *Alexander*, on the Skeena River. She was launched in 1875 and was put to work towing ships to and from Cape Flattery, primarily those headed for the Nanaimo coal docks. Being expensive to run, she soon bankrupted her owners.

In 1876, Moodyville mill purchased the *Etta White*, which had been built in Puget Sound. She was one of the first steam tugs in B.C. having a propeller drive, and was put to work towing ships in and out of Burrard Inlet since the *Isabel* had been sold to American operators to tow out of Victoria and Nanaimo.

The B.C. Towing and Transportation Company bought the *Beaver* in 1877 and entered the towing

9. The *Beaver* after she had her housework altered and was refitted with a new steam engine, Vancouver harbour, March 1888.

10. The steam tug *Isabel* photographed in Victoria harbour.

11. The mighty steam tug *Alexander*, built by the McAllister brothers, as she appeared in Victoria harbour, 1876.

business, with James Warren, a sealer-trader, as master. The company advertised her: "The powerful steam tug *Beaver*, fitted with two 36-inch cylinders, having been thoroughly overhauled and fitted with new boilers and other improvements, making her one of the most powerful and economical tugs on this coast, is now prepared to tow vessels in B.C. waters."

For most of the 1870s, towboating was very limited in scope. There were few tugs and only two jobs—towing lumber ships to the Hastings and Moodyville mills in Burrard Inlet or towing coal ships to Nanaimo. Hastings mill operated the *Isabel*, while Moody mills had the *Etta White*. The Victoria-based tugs were mainly occupied with Dunsmuir's coal operations, and there was a close association between Dunsmuir, Warren of B.C. Towing, and Captains Christensen, Marchant and Pamphlet. Warren eventually sold the tug *Pilot* to Dunsmuir, who also bought the *Alexander* from the McAllisters. Warren, Marchant and Christensen each served as master of the *Alexander* for a while.

The tugs built and used for towing ships in those days did not look at all like modern tugs. Long and narrow they were, with a deep draft, big propellers and more than 1,000 horsepower in their steam engines. These early tugs were big, almost the size of the sailing ships that they towed.

Even though the main task of towboats was to assist sailing ships in their approaches and departures from the coast, towboat owners and ships' agents had no idea when a ship would arrive off Cape Flattery. So, after a tug had towed a ship out, it had to wait for business in the vicinity of the cape. Precisely where it waited depended on a number of factors: who else was out there waiting, the tide, the wind, the time of year, and so on. If a brisk westerly was blowing up the strait, no ship's master would take a tow until he got up to Port Angeles or Victoria. If no wind was blowing and the ship was at the mercy of the tides and currents, its master would want to be picked up or cut loose as far from shore as possible, perhaps as far as seventy-five miles. And when a southeast gale was blowing up the coast, the ship's master would want to be at least fifteen miles offshore if he was dependent on the power of his own sails. When the conditions were just right, ships would come into a harbour such as Nanaimo or

Union Bay on their own, but usually they were towed in. Ships heading for Vancouver were almost always towed through the narrows by big tugs and dropped off at the ballast grounds. The ships carried ballast because they were not bringing in cargoes: the sparse population of the province did not create much demand for imported goods. The ballast, mostly sand, was unloaded by hand; then one of the smaller tugs working around the harbour moved the ships to loading piers.

Ship towing was a highly competitive business and the price charged depended upon the circumstances. Of course, towboats operated by coal companies or the export lumber mills were primarily concerned with providing fast and safe passage for the ships heading to their loading wharves. But other ships often used one of the many independent towboats or towing companies. Sailing ship captains could, on occasion, beat down the bids of competing towboat skippers. At other times, when a ship was sailing slowly but surely stern first onto the Vancouver Island shore, the only towboat in sight was in an excellent bargaining position.

In theory, the tug that towed in a ship got the contract to tow it back out when the time came. The practice, however, was a different matter because of the laws protecting national interests. For instance, a Canadian tug might pick up a ship and take it into Seattle, but the law would not allow it to tow the ship out so an American tug would get the job. And if an American tug towed a ship into Vancouver, the law would require a Canadian tug to tow it out to sea.

As construction proceeded at a steady pace in Vancouver and Victoria, and as export markets grew, the two mills on Burrard Inlet became very busy. The problem was that wharves were in short supply. Moreover, it took about two months to stow lumber in the covered hold of a sailing ship, which meant a long wait for berths. The solution was timesaving and economical. Ships began to load from lighters or from scows which tugs towed out from the mills.

The tugs that were used to move scows within the confines of a harbour did not have to be as large and powerful as those used for towing ships. A few smaller tugs were built locally or were bought from Americans. The *Mamie*, owned by J.F.T. Mitchell of Seattle, was

12

13

12. The steam-powered, propeller-driven tug *Etta White* on the Fraser River at New Westminster circa 1900.

13. Another famous tug of the time, the *Pilot*, at Victoria circa 1890. She was then owned by coal baron Robert Dunsmuir.

launched in New Westminster in 1878. George Cavin, once a master of the *Beaver*, bought the *Hope* in Port Townsend and went into business for himself. Other tugs operating then were the *Woodside*, built at Sooke for a Captain Trenchard, and the *Maggie*, owned by Jeremiah Rogers and captained by George Gilley. Gilley had just arrived from New Brunswick and was soon joined by his three brothers and their father. The Gilleys were to build a diversified farming, towing, fuel and building materials business.

The period between Confederation and completion of the Canadian Pacific Railway in 1885 was not one of particularly rapid development in B.C. Presumably many investors were waiting for the railway to begin operations. However, the forest and mining industries had become established and found export markets. Harbour facilities had been constructed to deal with increased shipping. Towboats had proved their worth as an essential part of the water transportation system, and the use of scows and barges had begun. The province was prepared to take advantage of the opportunities that a transcontinental railway would bring.

The Harbor

14. Hastings mill store wharf in 1886. The name board of Jeremiah Rogers's old tug *Maggie* is nailed to the boathouse wall, the paddle-wheel tug *Mermaid* is on the ways, and the barge *Robert Kerr* is in the stream.

3 / River of Logs, Fish and Coal

The completion of the Canadian Pacific Railway in 1885 contributed to the growth of Vancouver as an international port and had a dramatic effect on the resource and industrial development of British Columbia. The activity was centred on Burrard Inlet and quickly spread up the coast. Soon, a river of logs, coal and fish—a resource newly developed on a commercial scale—was beginning to flow into Burrard Inlet from a network of outlying operations. These undertakings generated a need for water transport, and it was in this period that the towing industry began to use log booms and increased its use of barges.

The fifteen years between the arrival of the railway and the turn of the century were an exciting time of expansion. Everything seemed to be happening at once. Small harbours were becoming international ports. Logging camps, mills, mines and canneries were popping up along the coast, to harvest the riches of land and ocean. The inside waters of the B.C. coast were becoming a busy marine highway for sailing ships, coastal steamers and oceangoing steamships, and for tugs of all sizes towing booms and barges.

One of the major reasons for constructing the railway was to provide the central link in a sea-and-land route between Britain and the Orient. The CPR chartered three old Cunard liners, the *Abyssinia*, the *Parthia* and the *Batavia*, to launch a regular passenger and freight service between Vancouver and the Orient. When the CPR obtained a lucrative mail contract in 1889, it began building the Empress ships: the *Empress of India*, the *Empress of China* and the *Empress of Japan*.

15. The historic arrival of the *Empress of India* in 1891, the first of the CPR's famed "white liners" to reach Vancouver.

15

16

16. The *Spratt's Ark* in Vancouver harbour on Dominion Day, 1890.

In addition to passengers, CPR steamships carried cargoes of tea and silk. On arrival in Vancouver, these goods were off-loaded directly onto trains that had right of way over all other traffic, were rushed to Montreal and New York, and there were loaded onto ships for the Atlantic crossing. Shipping activity increased even more in 1893 when the Canadian-Australian Steamship Company launched the All-Red Trans-Pacific Service to link Britain with its dominions in the Pacific.

As a result of the growth of shipping and the completion of the railway, more coal had to be barged to Vancouver from mines on Vancouver Island, in order to fuel steam-powered ocean liners and railway locomotives. A number of tugs were used for this task, including the *Pilot*, the *Beaver* and the *Spratt's Ark*, one of the strangest vessels ever to ply the coastal waters. She had been launched in Victoria in 1883 by a well-known shipbuilder, Joseph Spratt. The design was basically that of a scow, 220 feet long and 40 feet wide. She had two steam engines and twin propellers and had originally been intended for use as a floating cannery off the west coast. When this venture failed, the owners attempted to recoup the $75,000 cost of the *Spratt's Ark* by putting her to work freighting coal, rocks and gravel—both on her own decks and in scows towed behind—thus qualifying her as one of the area's early towboats.

The export market for coal had also grown

considerably and, by the 1890s, Robert Dunsmuir's Vancouver Island mines were shipping out 400,000 tons of coal a year, most of it to fuel the growing Pacific steamship fleet and for domestic or industrial use in the west coast towns of the United States. It was common at this time to see ten or twelve ships anchored in Departure Bay near Nanaimo, waiting to load. Farther north at Union Bay, the harbour was equally busy.

Although the number of steamships was increasing, the many sailing ships requiring assistance to and from Cape Flattery provided full-time work for several tugs. The most famous of them was the *Lorne,* built by Robert Dunsmuir in 1889. Her first master was James Christensen. She was destined to

play a leading role in the lives of people and in the events central to the marine history of the coast.

A son of Charles H. Cates, Jim, described a day when he was out on the *Lorne*. The sun was shining and a brisk afternoon westerly was blowing up Juan de Fuca Strait. Plowing through the cresting waves were rank after rank of great sailing ships: schooners, barques and brigs, dozens of them, all canvas set, driving before the wind at about 18 knots. They were headed for Vancouver, Victoria, Union Bay, Nanaimo, Seattle and Tacoma. There was not the sound of an engine to be heard: just the hissing and splashing of the water, the creaking of the rigging and the wooden hulls, the popping of canvas sails and the shouts of

17

17. The classic tug *Lorne* with some of her crew members on deck, circa 1925 when she was owned by Hecate Strait Towing.

18. The *Gleeful* tied up alongside a log boom in the 1940s. The 73.4-foot tug was built in Vancouver in 1913. Coastal Towing bought her from Canadian Western Lumber in 1946; in 1964 she was converted into a floating fish camp.

sailors in what, by then, had turned into a wild race through the strait. And not one of them was at all interested in taking a towboat before reaching Royal Roads or Port Townsend.

But the situation would be quite different when a gale hit. Then the *Lorne* would have to fight her way back to harbour after releasing an outward-bound ship well offshore. She would have to drag her five-inch-thick towline for forty miles before her crew could manage to get out on the aft deck to start up the steam capstan and haul in the line.

One day in the early 1890s, the *Lorne* was cruising through the fog between Cape Flattery and Carmanah Point on Vancouver Island. She came upon a ship out of Liverpool, bound for Burrard Inlet to pick up a load of lumber. This ship had been at sea for 180 days and, lost in the fog, was slowly drifting onto the beach. The crew was elated at the sight of the *Lorne*, which took them in tow to Royal Roads, where the two boats tied up together. All hands, who had been eating salted horse meat and hardtack for six months, were invited on board the *Lorne* for a dinner of ham, roast beef, fresh bread and pies. A young apprentice on that ship was Barney Johnson. Thirty years later he owned his own towboat fleet, including the *Lorne*.

The lumber industry was one of the first to feel the influence of the railway. Vast amounts of lumber were needed to build the railway itself: ties, snowsheds, bridges, stations and other buildings. At the same time, a booming export market was developing in South America, Australia, China and England.

The railway brought with it a flood of eastern investors, businessmen, speculators and promoters, many of whom established sawmills on the Fraser River, Burrard Inlet, False Creek and in Victoria. John Hendry took over Hastings mill and some smaller operations and reorganized them all under the name of B.C. Mills Timber and Trading Company. Eventually, this company bought out the Moodyville Sawmill Company.

By the mid-1880s most of the established sawmills had begun to run out of timber that could be skidded to the mill site. They began to acquire timber leases farther along the beach or up the coast, and had to tow the logs from the logging camps to the mills. As the mills went farther afield to get logs, they had to devise methods to move large quantities of logs. In protected waters, flat-booming was the procedure used. Large logs, straight and sound, called boomsticks, were bored with holes and chained together to form long, narrow rectangular enclosures. The width of a boom was between 66 feet and 70 feet, the standard length of a boomstick. The sides of a boom varied from one to many boomsticks, or sidesticks, depending on the length of the boom. The logs to be towed were then stowed lengthwise within the boom. At the junction of each sidestick, a cross-log or swifter was placed widthwise over the top of the contained logs and chained to the corresponding junction on the other side of the boom. The area in the square created by the swifters and sidesticks—about 70 feet a side—was known as a section. A boom might be many sections long and, in later years, booms were chained together side by side to create massive eighty-section tows, three to four booms wide.

After they had been made up at a logging camp, booms were picked up by tugs and taken to the mills. They could not be pulled very fast or the logs would begin to roll out or the boomsticks might break or something else would go wrong. The usual towing speed was one or two knots, depending on the weather. If the wind gusted to over 25 or 30 knots, tugs pulled into protected areas to wait for calmer weather. During the winter, it might be weeks before the conditions improved enough for towing. Eventually, certain spots where it was convenient to tie up logs became well used, and often half a dozen tugs and their booms were tied up in the same cove for two or three weeks.

One such location was Ragged Islands, just off Lund. This was very convenient because in later years there was a beer parlour at Lund. As might be expected, there were also beer parlours at other strategic locations. On the other side of the Yuculta Rapids, where a log tower would often have to wait for slack tide, was the Shoal Bay bar. And at the mouth of Knight Inlet, a bit farther north, was the Minstrel Island beer parlour.

The boats that towed booms often had to be built to order, since boats like the *Isabel* or the *Lorne*, which were used to tow ships, were too powerful to tow logs. At full power, the *Lorne* would have pulled a boom apart. Yet the smaller tugs that were beginning to operate around the harbours were not powerful enough.

Some of the older, less powerful ship-towing tugs were used successfully to tow booms. The *Beaver*, in fact, was engaged in some of the first coastal log towing under George Marchant, who was among the first, if not the first to negotiate a log boom through the Seymour and Yuculta rapids. The *Beaver* usually left Vancouver with a load of supplies for the upcoast logging camps, stopped at Nanaimo for coal, and proceeded north to East Thurlow Island where the supplies were unloaded and a tow of logs was picked up for Hastings mill.

A September 1883 edition of the *Victoria Evening Post* contained the following account of the *Beaver*'s log-towing activities:

The steamer *Beaver*, Captain Jagers, arrived from Chemainus about 5:30 last evening, towing what was probably the largest boom of logs ever seen here or on the Sound. It measured 100 feet in width and was 800 feet long . . . The Beaver left Chemainus on Thursday morning last, but had to anchor two nights, owing to the thick and foggy weather. She reached the entrance to this harbor yesterday afternoon, without a single mishap or the loss of a log. Some little difficulty was experienced in steering the mammoth raft into the harbor, two men being stationed on the structure for that purpose; but Capt. Jagers succeeded in skillfully navigating his cumbersome tow, and bringing it to its destination at Rock Bay, near Sayward's sawmill.

19

19. The steel-hulled *Tepic* (Evans, Coleman and Evans) tied up alongside a coal tipple and scow in 1914 or 1915.

On the night of 26 July 1888, the *Beaver* was leaving Vancouver harbour for Nanaimo to pick up a load of bunker coal before heading up to Johnstone Strait for a boom of logs. Coming through First Narrows she encountered a situation graphically described by Charles W. Cates:

There is a condition near Prospect Point which I think I should call attention to. This is the meeting of the back eddy with the ebb stream. As a big ebb pours out under the Lions Gate Bridge and flows toward Hollyburn, a strong back eddy is formed which runs along the shore from Siwash Rock towards Prospect Point....

My father used to tell me how the steamer "Beaver" ... was wrecked just south of Prospect bluff. She was a side-wheeler, with the rudder placed in the same position as an ordinary vessel. With her speed of 4 knots it meant that the rudder had very little effect. My father also said that on that trip the crew were sober and therefore not normal. However, she came slowly out of the narrows, and to dodge the tide rip the captain swung her bow to the south. As soon as the eddy struck her starboard bow she was swung to port and ran ashore just west of Prospect Point.

That was the end of the *Beaver*, the first boat on the coast to be used for towing. But by the time she went on the rocks, she had helped to prove the worth of towboats in dealing with the particular conditions encountered on the coast of British Columbia.

Soon there were not enough log-towing tugs

available to handle the output from upcoast logging camps, so the bigger mills began to build and operate their own. Also, by the late 1880s and early 1890s, significant numbers of independent handloggers were beginning to move into the multitude of small bays, inlets and coves of the inside waters. They sold their logs to mills in Vancouver, New Westminster and Victoria, and tugs were needed to take out their logs as well as to bring in their mail and supplies.

By the turn of the century, a number of tugs were moving booms down the coast. In 1888, the Moodyville mill contracted with Evans, Coleman and Evans, a Vancouver coal and building materials supplier, for the services of the *Tepic*. She was a steel-hulled steam tug built on the Thames for a French company working on the Panama Canal. George Marchant, who had been a skipper on the *Beaver*, was master, and the tug was put to work towing booms from Gulf Point. The Moodyville mill also used the *Etta White* to tow logs.

In 1889, Hastings mill had the *Active* built to tow logs. It already had the *Comet* and the *Belle* towing booms from its logging camps on East Thurlow Island. For a brief period, Hastings mill operated its tugs through a subsidiary called B.C. Mills Tug and Barge Company. In addition, the Royal City Mill operated the tug *Gipsy* out of New Westminster, while the Brunette Sawmill acquired the *Blonde*, the *Iris* and the *Vulcan* to work with the *Brunette*, which had been built in 1890.

20. The long-lived *Active* in Vancouver harbour circa 1905 when she was owned by Hastings mill.

In the late 1890s, log-towing rates between Howe Sound and Burrard Inlet ranged between $0.20 and $0.50 per thousand board feet; from the Yuculta Rapids, $0.75 to $1.00 a thousand board feet; and from above the Yucultas, up to $1.25 a thousand. To have a scow shifted cost $5.00, and to have a sailing ship towed from Cape Flattery to Vancouver was worth $200 to $250.

Salmon fishing could not be regarded as an industry in B.C. until the 1880s. Although the Hudson's Bay Company conducted some small-scale salting operations, salmon was used mainly for home consumption. Around 1871, farmers in the lower Fraser Valley began experimenting with hermetically sealed cans, and a few years later canneries were being established on the Fraser River. In 1882, Rivers Inlet Cannery was opened and within a few more years similar operations existed on the Skeena River. Eventually there were more than a hundred salmon canneries between the Fraser and the Skeena.

The transportation requirements of the new canning industry were enormous. Since, to conserve fish stocks, net fishermen were not allowed to use power-driven boats, their fishing boats had to be towed from one area to another, to the fishing grounds at the beginning of the week and back to the cannery at the end of the week. More transportation was needed to collect the fish from the boats, take it to the canneries, then to haul the cases of canned fish from the canneries to Vancouver and Victoria, from where it was exported.

Even as the towing industry was becoming established, the sea began to take its toll. In June 1892, the cannery tug *Standard*, owned by John Irving and R.P. Rithet of Victoria, was en route to Skeena River for the summer season when it went down in the tiderips off Cape Mudge. Five men died. Less than two years later, in the same spot, the *Estelle* foundered and eight men died. The *Estelle* was a Nanaimo-built log tower owned in part by the mayor, Andrew Haslam, and was on her way to the Rock Bay area with supplies and to pick up a boom.

Naturally this thriving coastal industry and shipping activity stimulated development of the province's principal harbours—Vancouver, Victoria and New Westminster. By 1900 Vancouver harbour had expanded to include False Creek and English Bay.

21. The Cates shipyard circa 1900. George Cates, owner (*2nd from l.*), his son Adrian (child in *centre*), and his father Andrew Jackson Cates, cobuilder of one of the earliest log rafts (*3rd from r.*). The *Robert Dunsmuir* is on the ways for repairs.

22. Five lumber ships loading from the dock at
Hastings mill circa 1890.

23. The cannery tug *Delta* tied up alongside salmon
    scows circa 1890.

Boatyards and sawmills were in full swing at a number of locations in the harbour. Charles H. Cates's brother, George, arrived and set up a boatyard in False Creek. Alfred "Andy" Wallace, a young boatbuilder from England, came to Vancouver in 1889 and started building fish boats, also in False Creek. During the following year the CPR built six stern-wheelers there to service the Klondike trade.

Wharves were under construction along the south shore of Burrard Inlet around the site of the Hastings mill. The CPR had its docks at the foot of Granville Street, the end of steel, and the city put in a wharf just east of it. Evans, Coleman and Evans built an enormous wharf at the foot of Columbia Street. Loading and unloading at these new facilities were tugs with barges and a small fleet of coastwise steamers moving passengers and freight to and from the upcoast logging camps and canneries, with connections to Victoria, Nanaimo and Puget Sound. But the really heavy work of towing fish boats and collecting fish was done by boats built specifically for the job. Some of these were fish packers, which had large holds; they collected the fish from the small net boats and hauled the fish to the cannery. Many of these packers were also used to tow the fish boats. But most canneries also built tugboats, which did not have holds in which to pack fish, but instead towed a collecting scow.

A typical cannery tug of this era was the *Swan*. She was a 45-foot steam tug built at Rivers Inlet in 1891 by the manager of the Rivers Inlet Cannery, Bob Drainey. When Drainey left to set up his own cannery at Namu, he took the *Swan* with him. After performing a variety

24. An unidentified tug at a logging camp in Port Essington, between 1900 and 1910.

of tasks all over the coast for many decades, the *Swan* wound up on the Fraser River, where she is still working.

As more and more sawmills, logging camps, mines and canneries came into operation along the coast, a larger volume of raw materials, finished products, equipment and supplies had to be transported. Sailing ships could not be used, for their lack of manoeuvrability put them at risk; in fact, they had to be towed to and from Cape Flattery. Steamships needed wharf facilities to load and unload freight of any bulk or weight, because of the 15- to 20-foot tidal ranges common on the coast. However, even the major harbours were short of wharves, and only a few of the logging, mining and cannery operations on the coast had them. The barge or scow had already been used successfully for barging coal and lumber and it had a number of advantages. A barge was inexpensive and simple to construct. It was open, rather than having a hold, so loading and unloading were faster and easier. And it could conveniently be dropped off and left for loading for as long as necessary, while the tug carried on with other jobs.

The growth of New Westminster as a port was different because of its location twenty-two miles up the Fraser River. Until a channel was dredged up the South Arm in 1885, there was only eight feet of water at low tide. The shallowness of the river and the speed of the currents during the freshet months of May to August discouraged sailing ships from coming into New Westminster for lumber.

The river, did, however, have one real advantage to offer mill owners. The fresh water inhibits the growth of teredos and other marine borers which can destroy a log boom in a matter of weeks. Because a sawmill requires large and safe storage areas to maintain an adequate log inventory, the Fraser was recognized as a good location, and during the 1890s about twenty mills were operating in New Westminster. In 1891 the Ross-Mclaren mill opened; within a few days the *Active* appeared towing the barque *Myra*, which loaded 600,000 feet of lumber bound for Australia. A decade later, as Fraser River Saw Mills, it became the largest lumber mill in the British Empire, cutting up to 400,000 board feet a day.

Although the big export mills tended to locate in

Burrard Inlet, a large volume of lumber was provided by mills on the Fraser River. It was soon common practice for the ships to anchor or tie up in Burrard Inlet and for lumber to be delivered to them on scows towed by tugs from New Westminster and False Creek. In addition to this work, there were a myriad of other tasks for towboats to perform in the harbour—moving ships after they had unloaded their ballast, hauling building materials, tending dredges and pile drivers, and ferrying passengers across the inlet. Consequently, a fleet of harbour boats began to evolve that were quite different from those towing ships or logs; they were shorter and narrower, and had less powerful engines and smaller crews.

One of the first of these harbour craft, which could only loosely be called a towboat, was an amazing sight. An old threshing machine engine was mounted on an even older scow, paddle wheels were placed on each side and she was launched as the *Union*. She had one gear, forward; and one speed, full ahead. The paddle wheels were chain driven, and the throttle wire occasionally broke, to the detriment of the harbour's pilings and wharves, thereby earning the boat the nickname "Sudden Jerk." George Marchant, who was captain for a time, devised a makeshift but effective method of stopping. He kept a pile of gunny sacks handy and tossed them into the chain drives of the paddle wheels whenever the throttle wire broke.

Eventually, the *Union* was bought by the Moodyville mill, and some cautious soul attached a chain to the engine with a buoy at the other end, to save the engine in the somewhat likely event that it fell through the boat's bottom.

Fortunately for the future of B.C.'s marine industries, conventional harbour craft were also constructed. One of the inlet's first towboat companies, the Burrard Inlet Towing Company, was established in 1886. When it reorganized itself as the Union Steamship Company in 1890, it owned three boats, two of them originally built for James Van Bramer. The *Leonora*, a 57-foot propeller-driven steamboat, was built in Victoria by Spratt. The 51-foot *Senator* was

25. The steamboat *Leonora* was used for occasional towing and ferrying passengers. She was built for Capt. James Van Bramer who named her after his two daughters Louisa and Nora.

built in Moodyville in 1881 by Henry Maloney, and the third, the 76-foot tug *Skidegate*, was built in 1879. All three of these boats carried passengers to and from various points in the inlet and it is generally thought that they also undertook towing jobs. However, Claude Thicke, who came to Vancouver as a nine-year-old in 1892 and spent his spare time paddling around the harbour on a plank with an apple box nailed on for a seat, does not remember ever seeing the *Senator* towing anything.

James Van Bramer also had a small tug called the *Chinaman*, which had been brought from the Orient on the deck of a sailing ship. Another imported vessel was the *Nagasaki*, a rather luxurious steam launch built

in Japan for A.G. Ferguson, the city's park commissioner and an official of the CPR. She was made of teak, with copper fastenings, and had a tastefully upholstered interior. Like many other boats, she ended up towing to earn her keep, primarily moving scows around the harbour and the bottom end of the Strait of Georgia.

Although Victoria had been eclipsed by Vancouver as the centre of industrial development on the coast, its status as a port city rose during the later years of the nineteenth century. The Esquimalt dry dock, which had been built as part of the Confederation agreement, was operating at full tilt. A number of shipyards, of which the most eminent was Joseph Spratt's, were building

26. The private steam launch *Nagasaki* in Vancouver harbour circa 1890. She was built in Japan for A.G. Ferguson, after whom Ferguson Point in Stanley Park is named.

boats and servicing the deep-sea fleet.

The marine atmosphere in Victoria was noticeably different from that of Vancouver. Much of Vancouver's marine activity was focussed on the harbour itself, as well as on the inside waters of Puget Sound and the Strait of Georgia. Victoria, on the other hand, was a cosmopolitan Pacific port. Its large seafaring population looked more towards the deep sea than to the inside waters. The existence of a dry dock at nearby Esquimalt and the neighbouring naval base brought to the city the smells, sounds and people of world shipping. In 1894, for example, 1,394 deep-sea vessels entered her harbour; whereas even in 1901, only 71 oceangoing vessels called at Vancouver.

The ownership of towboats at this time lay mostly with those who used them: lumber mills, canneries and mines which, with few exceptions, rarely set up separate companies for their boats. There was no connection between them and the independent towboat industry that began to develop at the end of the century.

These company-owned tugs were not entirely able to keep up with the proliferating demands made on them and, as work and financing became available for ambitious, hard-working young men willing to take the chances involved in going into business for themselves, the independent towboat industry began. These independent operations were small, usually an individual with a boat or two.

26

27

27. The *Czar* was built in Victoria in 1897 for Hastings mill. Photographed before she got a Bolinder diesel engine in 1923.

Capt. G.H. French, considered the first independent log tower to operate out of Vancouver, started with the *Huron* during this era. Charles H. Cates, who appears to have been involved in just about everything happening in Vancouver harbour, had owned and disposed of three tugs by 1900—the *Swan* (the second tug with this name), the *Lois* and the *Stella*—then went into the pile-driving business, though he eventually returned to towing. George McKeen in New Westminster had the *Stranger* and a few scows which he ran on the Fraser. Also on the Fraser, the Gilley brothers had a tug called the *Flyer* towing sand and gravel barges. Harold Jones began towing in 1898 with the *On Time* and the *Uncle Tom*. One of the larger fleets assembled belonged to an engineer named N.R. Preston and Capt. George F. Mann. They owned the *Fearless,* the *Dauntless*, the *Peerless*, the *Faultless*, the *Earl*, and, later, the *Robert Preston*. Their company came to be called Preston-Mann. There were, of course, many more towboaters steaming around the province's coastal waters in their tugs. The men and companies named here, however, formed part of the foundation of the independent towing companies that are in operation today.

28. The *Fearless* as she looked fifty years after being built. The photograph was taken when she was owned by Coastal Towing.

4 / *The Timber Boom*

During the first few years of this century a series of events occurred in other parts of the continent that were to have an enormous effect on the economy of British Columbia. First, the Ontario and Quebec governments decided to prohibit the export of logs from Crown lands, in order to halt the increasing sales to eastern U.S. mills, which had depleted most of their own timber reserves. Then, in 1901, Theodore Roosevelt brought in stringent conservation legislation to protect U.S. forests. These two measures forced American mills to look elsewhere for logs. They did not have to search hard: long-term, renewable timber leases were available for a token rental in British Columbia. Over a two-year period, more than fifteen thousand of these leases were granted. A number of investors also took advantage of the pulp leases established in 1901 to encourage the construction of the pulp and paper mills. The Americans had arrived, and the timber boom was on.

One of the early American pulp and paper operations was Brooks-Scanlon at Stillwater. After acquiring the Powell River pulp lease in 1909, Brooks-Scanlon began construction of what was to become the world's largest newsprint mill. At about the same time, a number of railway builders and lumbermen from Bellingham, Washington, organized a Canadian company to engage in timber speculation and logging —Bloedel, Stewart and Welch. This company obtained large timber leases just north of Stillwater, as well as a shingle mill on the Fraser River and the Great Central Sawmill on Vancouver Island.

On Vancouver Island, the Cameron brothers took

over a mill in Victoria and also established the largest mill on the island, the Genoa Bay Lumber Company, at Cowichan Bay. Farther up-island, the Comox Logging and Railway Company, a division of the Canadian Western Lumber Company, was pioneering the use of steam donkeys and logging railways—techniques imported from the United States along with investment dollars. Also involved in the early use of logging railways was the Victoria Lumber and Manufacturing Company at Chemainus, the island's other major operator.

By 1910, there were about 250 sawmills in the province, most of the major ones being located on the coast. There were also about 350 logging camps, many of them equipped with the latest in high-production steam equipment. Comox Logging, the largest operation in the province, took 120 million board feet a year out of its Vancouver Island camp.

The growing number of logging camps and sawmills and the scale of their activities resulted in large volumes of logs and lumber that needed to be transported. The emphasis of the towing industry slowly began to shift to the forest industry during this time, a shift which also recognized that steamships were replacing sailing ships. The future of the big ship-towing tugs that escorted sailing ships in from the open sea seemed uncertain. Both mining and canning operations, however, continued to prosper and used a

29. Sailing ship docked at Hastings mill circa 1900. Unidentified tug in foreground with manila towline coiled in stern.

large number of tugboats.

By the turn of the century the fishing industry had completed its pioneering phase. Scores of small canneries had been established on the Fraser and Skeena rivers, Rivers Inlet and numerous other locations along the coast. In 1901, a record-breaking sockeye run on the Fraser attracted worldwide attention in the form of increased export orders and investment capital. Over the next year, more than half of the canning facilities on the coast were bought up by B.C. Packers with money from eastern Canada. In that year 1.2 million cases of salmon were canned. Similar takeovers on a smaller scale consolidated most of the remaining canneries within another three or four years. During the same period the introduction of purse seines and gasoline-powered boat engines opened up fishing grounds farther away from the mouths of the major spawning rivers.

During the peak of this activity a hundred or so towboats worked for or were owned by canneries. These tugs performed a variety of tasks. They transported supplies, fishermen and cannery workers to the canneries at the opening of the season; towed fish boats out to the fishing grounds and back, and towed scows to collect the catch each day and take it to the canneries.

Possibly the busiest area for fishing industry towboats was around the Skeena River. In the early

1900s, the ban on gas-powered fishing boats was lifted in all waters except the Skeena, where it remained in force for a number of years. For a twenty-year period there were thirteen or fourteen canneries on the Skeena, each with 65 to 125 fish boats that needed towing. Initially, these boats were towed out onto the Skeena at night and picked up in the morning, when the fish were loaded into a scow brought along for that purpose. In later years the fish boats began to move out of the river as far as Hecate Strait.

When fishing was restricted to the river, most of the tugs used were steam-powered and relatively small —40 to 60 feet long. They included the *Florence* and the *Spray* at Inverness cannery, the *Vera* at Cassiar, the *Eva* and the *Bamberton* chartered by Oceanic, the *Claxton* at Claxton, and the *Clive* and the *Hong Kong* at Carlysle.

As the fishing grounds were extended out into the coastal waters, larger towboats were required. Cunninghams cannery acquired the *Chieftain* and the *Lottie N.* The *Tyee*, built for B.C. Packers, was one of the more unusual-looking tugs on the coast. She had the lines of a war canoe, including a long pointed bow carved with tribal emblems. Unfortunately her engine's rotation was opposite to the normal, so that she backed to starboard instead of to port when making a landing. The result was that her fancy bowsprit suffered numerous collisions with pilings and was eventually

30

30. The *Haro* towing in a sailing ship circa 1920. Built at Hastings mill for its subsidiary B.C. Mills Tug and Barge, which merged with M.R. Cliff Tugboat in 1932. In 1957 she went to Vancouver Tug Boat and was renamed the *Le Beau*.

31

These were all steam-powered tugs, but gradually gas-powered boats began to appear on the Skeena. The first was the *Oceanic* at Oceanic cannery, followed by the *Totem* and the *Kyak* at Balmoral, the *Linde* at Cassiar, the *Adam* and the *Eve* at North Pacific, the *Klatawa* at Dominion, and the *Nahmint* at Claxton.

Don Peck, who served as master on a number of these tugs, once wrote an account of those days:

When the boats were picked up . . . they were towed on two towlines, with splice-in beckets every 30-odd feet, so that when the tug got under way she had two strings of boats in pairs for the length of her tow. When I towed the boats for Cassiar we would have 30 or so boats on each string.

worn down to a stub.

32

31. The *Haro* at Hastings mill dock in the 1920s.

32. 33. The cannery tug *Tyee* towing fish boats for Balmoral Cannery, Port Essington, 1900. Two views: one from the fish boats (*l.*) and one from

When the mouth of the river was reached we would set a course outside of Holland Rock (no lighthouse then) and bear off towards Eddye Pass until a more less mid-sound position was reached, when we would bear off toward Rachel Island. The boats would be dropping off along the way wherever the fishermen's fancy dictated, so, by the time we reached Rachel Island, they would all have to let go and the tug would put about and head for Humpback Bay on Porcher Island to anchor for the night. The tugs would leave the harbor early enough in the morning to get down to the leeward boats when they picked up their nets at daylight.

There was no fishing in these waters in the daylight hours as the water was so clear the fish could see the nets and avoid them. Picking up the boats in the morning was a much more complex problem than towing them out in the evening as they were invariably scattered far and wide, especially if the wind had freshened during the night from the S.E.

Some of the boats might take shelter behind Lucy Island and I have seen the odd boat well out toward Triple Island before we were able to catch up with it. It was essential that none be missed, for if the southeaster prevailed they might not get back for days, their fish would spoil, and this situation invariably led to a long and expensive search.

The coastal mining industry also continued to flourish during the first decades of the century. The Anyox copper mine on Observatory Inlet was by far the largest operation, supporting a population of 2,500 by 1920. Large copper mines were also operating at

the stern of the tug (r.). She was built in New Westminster in 1899 and was lost in a gale in Juan de Fuca Strait in 1923.

34. The City Wharf Company dock, Vancouver. Tugs include, *l. to r.: Naiad, Canadian, Hopkins, Daisy, Tepic, Squid, Native, Stetson,* *B.C. Maid, Imp, Dauntless, Wireless, Esdud* and the dredge *Mastodon.*

Vananda, Alice Arm and Surf Inlet; dozens of smaller ones were scattered along the coast. Almost all of these declined during the 1920s or soon thereafter.

None of these copper mines, however, could compare in scale of operation to the Vancouver Island coalfields, which by this time stretched all the way from Comox to Ladysmith. Although the internal combustion engine powered by gas or oil was about to replace the coal-fired, steam-powered engine, steam was still the main motive force. And while it remained so, coal was king; and as long as coal was king, a major proportion of the towing business on the coast was derived from it. In 1905 the CPR bought the Esquimalt and Nanaimo Railway from the Dunsmuir family,

including the tugs *Czar* and *Escort No. 2*, and began towing its own railcar barges and coal scows between the island and Vancouver.

There was, at this time, an enormous increase in the coastal population. In addition to the cannery and mining centres already mentioned, pulp mills were established at Swanson Bay and Ocean Falls, and agricultural communities were begun at Cape Scott, Malcolm Island and dozens of other locations. Practically every piece of arable land and every bay or cove with fresh water between Lund and the Skeena River was settled—by a total of 15,000 or even 20,000 people.

This large coastal population, most of which was in

35. The *St. Clair*, one of the first steam tugs in B.C. to be converted to burning oil, was built in 1898 and sank in a gale in 1948.

place by 1920, was serviced by the Union Steamship Company and a fleet of towboats. The Union boats, operating on strict schedules, took care of the passenger and freight end of the transportation system. The tugs barged in the heavier equipment needed for logging and mining and took out the raw materials that had been produced—mostly logs headed for the mills in Vancouver, the Fraser, Puget Sound and Victoria.

As tugs began to tow more and more logs, the older towboat people, not particularly interested in log towing, began to leave the business. The younger men who had recently moved in as independent owner-operators began to expand their operations and were joined by others.

George French, who was already in the upcoast log-towing business with the *Huron*, acquired two more boats, the *St. Clair* and the *Superior*. The *St. Clair*, a 79-foot, 66-ton boat, had been built in New Westminster and was used for towing logs down the coast. The *Superior* was used in the harbour for moving booms around and for other general towing.

In 1902, the *Superior* was on her maiden voyage under the command of George Marchant, who appears to have been the master of every tug afloat at the time. It was bringing a tow of logs in through First Narrows with the tide. When Marchant cut into the back eddy at Brockton Point to head into Coal Harbour, the boom took over and dragged the *Superior* under. All hands

35

were saved and the tug was later raised. The Vancouver *Province* dryly noted that not only had Marchant succeeded in sinking the *Beaver*, the coast's oldest vessel, just outside the harbour in 1888 but he had also just sunk the newest one.

In 1905, French had Charles Robertson build the *Sea Lion*, probably the classic log-towing boat. In addition to her power and her seaworthiness, the boat was designed with the comfort of the crew in mind. She had a spacious salon, equipped with a piano; and the whistle had a sliding scale upon which the crew played a somewhat haphazard repertoire of songs, learned and practised during the long tows down the coast.

The evolution of the French operation was a good example of what was happening. In 1902, Lloyd Gore, twenty-two years old at the time, had gone to work for French as an engineer and three years later installed the *Sea Lion*'s new steam engines. In 1909, Gore and Capt. Harry Young went into business for themselves and bought the *Superior* and the *St. Clair* from French, who began to get out of towboating and into the automobile business. The British Canadian Lumber Company bought the *Sea Lion*, the *Erin* and the *Shamrock*, and put Claude Thicke in charge of them because he had spent time around the yacht club. When British Canadian Lumber folded a few years later, the *Sea Lion* went to Young and Gore, who continued to expand their business for the next thirty years.

36. The *Shamrock* and her nine-man crew.

36

37

Claude Thicke

Former president, Blue Band Navigation

I went down to Pacific Coast Lumber Mills, where the Bayshore Inn is now, to keep the books. I got sixty dollars a month. They were purchased by the British Canadian Lumber Company, and the boss said, "How much are you getting?"

I said, "Sixty dollars."

He said, "From now on your pay is a hundred and fifty." Boy, that was something.

They bought the *Sea Lion* from French, the *Erin*—I don't know where they got her from—and the *Shamrock:* three tugs. And nobody in British Canadian Lumber knew anything about boats at all. Nobody knew how much to charge or what they should put on the bill, and they towed for others besides towing their own logs.

The boss came in one day, opened the door and said, "You've got to take over the tugs." I'd been in the yacht club and I'd been up and down the coast, so I knew most of the places our boats towed from. I was then in charge of the tugs, which was quite an experience.

Some of the crews would try to put it over on me, so they could stay in for the weekend or something. The *Sea Lion* was in one Friday, and the skipper came in and asked, "What's the orders?" I told him the orders. He said, "We can't leave for forty-eight, maybe seventy-two hours. The engineer tells me the air pump is busted."

I never knew if there was an air pump on a steam job, so I said, "Cap, I'll have to see about that." I telephoned the fellow who did our repairs and asked him, "What about this air pump on the *Sea Lion?*"

"Oh," he said, "she's pretty bad. It's got to be done right away." I figured he was in cahoots with the engineer, didn't want to get the engineer sore at him and go someplace else. So I had to tell him to go ahead and fix it. But I got hold of this international correspondence school and took a course in marine engineering. I wasn't going to have people tell me something I didn't know. I found out there was an air pump after I got on with it.

37. The classic tug *Sea Lion* in Vancouver harbour in 1914 when she was owned by Young and Gore.

In 1905, James Greer and E.J. Coyle established themselves in the towing business, but were not always looked upon very kindly by dedicated towboat people, as neither of them had a background in tugs. Both had been CPR employees—Greer in the freight division and Coyle in the passenger division. But they were in a good position to predict the future growth in coastal transportation needs and the potential of the towing business. So they plunged in and bought six tugs—the *Queen*, the *Stetson*, the *Owen*, the *Albion*, the *Achates* and the *Borden*—forming Greer and Coyle Towing. In the same year, Vancouver Tug and Barge Company was organized by George McDonald and Clarence Marpole. They soon built the *Dola*, a 350-horsepower steam tug, and the *Clayburn* with 200 horsepower.

In Victoria, George McGregor added two more boats to his Victoria Tugboats company, the *Spray* and the *Swell*. George Walkem, who owned the Vancouver Machinery Company, discovered one day that he had inadvertently become the owner of a well-used scow. He persuaded some friends to put up money and set up the Gulf of Georgia Towing Company. Their main business was moving lumber from the mills to ships anchored in the harbour. They soon acquired two tugs, the *Daring* and the *Ellison*, and more barges and initiated the practice of renting them out to other towboat operators. In the same year, 1912, Harold Jones gave his seventeen-year-old son a 60-foot tug, the *Rosina K*, with which young Harold set about establishing the beginnings of the Vancouver Tug Boat Company.

A further development around this time was that the lumber mills began to divest themselves of their towboat operations. However, leaving the towing to independent operators posed problems, particularly for the bigger mills. If they did not own their own tugs, the mills would be totally dependent on the towboaters for their log supply and, moreover, they would not have a reliable means of determining the actual costs of towing logs when it came time to negotiate towing rates. Consequently, the Powell River Company and Canadian Western Lumber Company established subsidiary companies in 1910—Kingcome Navigation and the Canadian Tugboat Company. These "captive" companies, as towboaters called them, remained firmly

under the control of the mills and their successors; for more than fifty years they were the only mill-owned towboat operations.

The other lumber companies all pulled out of the towing business. They sold their boats and turned their towing over to independent operators. There were a number of young and hungry towboat owners including Claude Thicke, who went into the business on his own. To start with—since he had no money—he chartered the *Plunger*. He made a bit of money on that and then got a chance to buy the *Coutli*. She was originally a Union Steamship tug and had been bought by McDowell and Mowatt to tow coal barges from Nanaimo and Union Bay to Vancouver. The company went broke and a bank took over the tug. Everyone in the business tried to talk Thicke out of buying the *Coutli* because she had a reputation as a heavy coal burner. He was convinced, however, that her engines should work better than they did and that they should burn less coal. He finally talked his engineer into drilling a few holes in the firebox door to get better combustion. It worked.

Claude Thicke soon acquired the *Phoenix* and then the *Maagen*. He was overseas during the war, but on his return got his master's ticket and took up towboating in a serious way. In 1920 he bought out the Progressive Steamboat Company, including its four tugs: the *Prosperative*, the *Pronative*, the *Prospective* and the *Projective*. He changed the company name to Blue Band Navigation. His first step was to convert some of his fleet to diesel.

For Vancouver in the early 1920s this was a radical

38. The *Stetson* circa 1905 when she was owned by Greer and Coyle Towing. She was one of the first tugs that the company bought.

move, as almost all the boats were powered by steam. Certainly, diesel had been tried already, but not very successfully. In fact, Thicke had been involved in building the first diesel tug, the *VN & T No. 1*, when he had been at the British Canadian Lumber Company. The tug had not worked well and then the war had come along. It was not until 1921 that the idea of using diesel engines began to circulate again.

Thicke was not alone in his belief in the diesel engine. G.H. French was converting a small navy tug to diesel, and John A. Cates was working on building the *Radio*, probably the first full-diesel tug to be made in Vancouver. But to take a whole fleet of tugs, all running well on perfectly reliable steam engines, and convert them to diesel was considered a pretty risky venture. Thicke did it and led what turned out to be a mass changeover to the new type of engine.

In Vancouver harbour the Cates family business was beginning to establish itself as one of the dominant marine forces, particularly in towboating. Charles H. Cates, having built the first wharf on the north shore of Burrard Inlet near the foot of Lonsdale Avenue, got back into the towing business in 1913 when he hired Andy Linton to build the *Gaviota*, still working almost seventy years later as the *C.H. Cates III*. By this time, his many brothers were also active. John A., who had various interests on Bowen Island and later ran a passenger service from there to Vancouver, owned two tugs, the *Radio* and the *Radius*. George, the False Creek shipbuilder, also owned a hotel in Howe Sound. Willard owned and operated the tug *Native*, which had a whistle with a sliding scale that earned him a fair reputation as a musician on the coast. And Jim, for a while, owned and operated the tug *Dominion*.

With the *Gaviota*, Charles H. Cates set up a towing company and brought his wife's brother, Henry Barrow, a marine engineer, into the business. Henry's brother, St. Clair Barrow, an accountant, also came in. During World War I, Charles's three sons—Charles Warren, John and Jim—went overseas. At this point it is easy to become confused about which Cates is which. The four daughters in the family stepped in to run the operation until the end of the war. And, of course, the sisters' husbands were towboaters who worked for the company. At the end of the war the sons returned and the company was renamed C.H. Cates & Sons.

Claude Thicke
Former president, Blue Band Navigation

When I bought the *Coutli* I had to have food for nine men for maybe a month. We might be away that long before we got in with a tow. I didn't know many of the suppliers very well. I knew Phil Malkin and Fred Malkin but they didn't want the business. So I went up to Bob Kelly.

I didn't know him then; a little short man, very quick in his decisions. I know I had stolen raisins from his boxes as a kid; if a box of raisins fell off a truck, we were all out there helping ourselves. One of those times he chased me up the street with a knife.

So I thought I'd go see Bob Kelly. I figured he couldn't stick a knife in me, because now he wasn't big enough. He was only a little one, about five foot two or three, and I was six foot one or two. I figured I could hold my own against him, so I went to see him.

Bob Kelly came up to me in his office and he said, "Well, boy, what do you want?"

So I said, "I bought the *Coutli* and I want nine hundred dollars credit from Kelly Douglas."

He said, "So how are you going to pay if off?"

I said I'd pay him in sixty days.

He just hollered to MacIntosh, "MacIntosh, give this boy what he wants."

And that's all there was to it.

39. The Blue Band Navigation fleet circa 1925, including the *Prosperative* and the *Projective*.

Claude Thicke

Former president, Blue Band Navigation

Buckley was the manager at British Canadian Lumber Company and decided there weren't enough tugs, so we built one, the *VN & T No. 1*—Vancouver Navigation and Towing Company. We put in a big eighty-horsepower engine, built in Holland and brought over here by Heeps. That was the first diesel tug on the coast, and everyone was against it.

If anything went wrong, it didn't matter what—if the towline broke or if it lost a boom on the way down —it was the fault of the diesel. If she broke down or got water in the fuel and happened to stop, they said, "Why there you are. That's what happens to diesel. It never happens to steam." They forgot that when you broke something in steam you stopped, too.

We sent her up to the end of Burrard Inlet to bring a boom down, and she burnt all the engine bearings out. It was still under guarantee so Heeps had to put them back in. Then we sent her down to bring some logs from San Juan to Victoria, and she burnt out a set of bearings again. Heeps wouldn't guarantee that, so we had to put them in. The bearings were huge things and cost too much money, so we just tied her up, didn't run her at all, because we found we could only tow six hours and out would go the bearings.

Then we got a clever engineer who'd had a bit of experience with diesels. "Instead of eighty horsepower," he said, "let's run her at sixty, and I'll clean the bearings out every eight or nine hours and it'll make money for you." He was right.

We wanted to change over one of our steam tugs to diesel, and the engineer quit. On the steam tug you could see the crank go up and down. You couldn't see it on the diesel. He said, "I can't see what I'm working on. I can't reach out and feel whether it's getting hot. I've got to see what I'm doing. I'm not working blind for anybody."

That's the kind of thing we ran up against.

In 1920, M.R. Cliff set up the M.R. Cliff Tugboat Company after obtaining the *Brunette* from Brunette mill. He acquired more boats, most of them from the various mills, and soon became the preeminent log tower on the coast.

Meanwhile, over on the Fraser River, a lot of logging, milling and towing activity had been taking place around New Westminster. In 1900, a mill that was eventually to become the Eburne Sawmill was established on the North Arm. Towing logs down the Fraser began when the British Canadian Lumber Company brought some booms from its camp near Yale down to its mill in Coal Harbour. Log towing from the upper river was limited to the freshet period when the

water was high and was undertaken by stern-wheelers, which usually spent their time working as freighters and ferries. Two boats that towed from the Yale area were the *R.P. Rithet* and the second *Beaver*. The *Skowlitz,* the *Firefly* and the *Gypsy* were also stern-wheelers towing out of Harrison Lake.

In 1912, the government started dredging out the North Arm, until then a shallow trickle of a stream at low tide. It had been eyed by mill owners and towboaters for a long time and must have been particularly appealing to the latter as they bucked a southeaster past its mouth at Point Grey, headed another four miles south to the main channel. By 1920, after the channel was dredged, twenty-five mills were

operating in the North Arm, and many tugs towing logs used this route on their way to mills farther up the river.

During this period the Fraser had become a busy marine highway and was the primary storage ground for logs. Mills in a variety of sizes were scattered along it all the way up to the Harrison River and logs were moving both up and down the Fraser.

Working the river above New Westminster has always been different from towing on the coast or even on the lower river. Upstream, the river is faster and shallower. It takes a boat drawing less than 10 feet of water to go above Port Mann, and one with a draft of less than 5 feet to work above Mission to Yale, the

40. The *Gryphon* photographed shortly after she was bought by Gulf of Georgia Towing. She was built in 1921 as the *Radio* by John Cates and was the first full-diesel tug built in Vancouver.

upper limit of navigation. Consequently, river tugs were smaller than coastal tugs.

Tides affect the Fraser River for fifty miles from its mouth at the Sandheads, as the area is called, as far up as Sumas. The tides, which at New Westminster have a 5-foot range, at the Sandheads have an average range of 12 feet. Tugs make good use of this tidal action, because the rising tide not only provides deeper water but also counteracts the force of the river current.

In those days a unique navigating system was used on the North Arm when it was necessary to travel at night. A rowboat was sent ahead with two men and a number of long poles and lanterns. As they felt out the channel, the men marked the turns by thrusting a pole into the sand with a lit lantern hanging from it. When the tug came along she followed this course, picking up the lanterns as she went.

The same kind of expansion in the towing industry that occurred on the coast also took place on the Fraser. The Gilley brothers' operation continued to grow; in 1905 they bought the *Robert Dunsmuir* and converted her to a tugboat. She had been built more than twenty years earlier as a side-wheel steamer by George Cates. Eventually she was converted into a twin-screw propeller vessel and spent some time carrying coal from Nanaimo, thus earning her the name "Dirty Bob."

John Hodder and his two sons got into the towing business when they bought the 57-foot steam tug *Hustler*, originally called the *Raven*. The Hodders installed a 75-horsepower Wolverine gas engine, reputed to be the first internal combustion engine placed in a B.C. tug.

Just after the war, Thomas Cooper bought the *Shuswap* and also went into business on the Fraser, operating with a number of other owner-operators from New Westminster as Cooper and Smith Towing. They, along with the Hodders, picked up whatever jobs they could: lumber, sand and gravel scows, and log booms. But by that time most of the towing on the river was being done by Vancouver outfits, primarily M.R. Cliff.

At the north end of the mainland coast, the completion of the Grand Trunk Pacific Railway in 1907 spelled the end of the settlements on the Skeena River and at Port Simpson, because the terminus was located at Prince Rupert on Kaien Island. Shortly thereafter, the Prince Rupert Towing Company was established

and in 1913 arranged with E.B. Schock of Vancouver to build the *PRT No. 1* with a two-cylinder Swedish-built Advance heavy oil engine of 92 horsepower, probably the first semi-diesel engine to be installed in a B.C. tug. Four years later, this engine was replaced with a 110-horsepower gasoline engine.

Around the turn of the century, the first salvage company in the province, B.C. Salvage, was organized in Victoria by A.C. Burdick. For a number of years this company operated the *Salvor* (a 215-foot steamship orginally called the *Danube*), the *Maud* and the *William Jolliffe*. This initial foray of a B.C. towboat firm into salvage and rescue was confined to the coastal waters. Until the development of ship-to-shore radio after the war, there was usually no way of knowing that a ship at sea was in trouble, so the company's major work consisted of pulling stranded ships off the rocks.

In 1911, for example, the *William Jolliffe* and the *Lorne* pulled the *Tees* off the beach in Barkley Sound. After B.C. Salvage was reorganized as Pacific Salvage in 1916, the *Tees* was purchased, refitted as a salvage tug and renamed the *Salvage Queen*. The *William Jolliffe*, which had been sold to the CPR and renamed the *Nitinat*, was bought back and renamed the *Salvage Chief*. These boats, along with the *Salvage King*, the *Burrard Chief* and the *Salvage Chieftain* (formerly the Coast Guard's *Lillooet*) established Pacific Salvage as the primary marine salvage and rescue concern in the north Pacific for the next thirty years until the company was merged with Straits Towing.

The hectic pace of industrial development that had been taking place along the coast since the late 1890s came to a sudden halt with the outbreak of World War I. Rumours of German battleships cruising the Pacific effectively shut down the export lumber market and a depression appeared to be settling in. Within months most of the 400 lumber mills and 800 logging camps in the province were in serious financial difficulties.

In time, however, the war created demands of its own. The first boost to the economy came with the passing of the Shipbuilding Assistance Act. Initially this was aimed at building schooners for hauling lumber but, as the Allied shipping losses increased, the Imperial Munitions Board began placing orders with B.C. shipyards for wooden steamers.

Part way through the war, the demand for airplane

41

spruce increased. Until the U.S. entered the war in 1917, most of the high quality spruce needed for aircraft construction had come from Washington and Oregon. But when the Americans required all their wood for their own planes, a search was begun in B.C. for spruce to build Canadian planes.

There were known to be spruce stands on the Queen Charlotte Islands, but they had never been cruised. Furthermore, there was virtually no logging in this part of B.C. because of the difficulties involved in towing logs across Hecate Strait.

A task force was set up, special legislation was passed, and within a year 400 logging contracts had been let. Logs were towed to five rafting centres, or to

42

41. The *Nitinat* and the *Transfer No.2*, a railcar barge, in 1920. The tug was built as the *William Jolliffe* in England in 1885.

42. *L. to r.*: the *Otter*, the *Dola* and the *Salvage King* in Vancouver circa 1930. Not the Hudson's Bay Company *Otter*.

one of the ten mills established in the Charlottes. Log rafts were constructed and logs towed to one of the seven mills cutting spruce between Ocean Falls and Prince Rupert. A fleet of eighteen tugs was assembled, including the *Massett* and the *Moresby* which were built by the Imperial Munitions Board specifically to tow logs.

The idea of the log raft did not originate on the west coast. It may have been started in Europe or on the Atlantic coast. In 1880 Charles H. Cates's father, Andrew Jackson Cates, was still in New Brunswick and undertook with a man named Robertson to build and move a raft of logs from New Brunswick to New York. The massive structure, about 600 feet long, a big cigar-

shaped object of logs chained and cabled together, was built on shore and launched like a ship. It was towed to a mill in New York harbour. Soon after this venture, Robertson moved west and built similar rafts in Washington and Oregon.

Several types of log rafts were eventually used in B.C. The best-known, and probably the first, was the Davis raft. One story has it that the raft was built to the specifications of Bert Davis, superintendent of the British Canadian Lumber Company camp on the west coast of Vancouver Island. It was towed to Tacoma by a Greer and Coyle tug. Another version of this historic event is that the *Sea Lion* made the first Davis raft tow,

43. The first log "crib" or raft to be towed across Hecate Strait. The raft was towed by the *Progressive* (Progressive Steamboat) for J.R. Morgan. Later the tug was bought by Kingcome Navigation and renamed the *D.A. Evans*.

but from Quatsino Sound in 1916 and with Davis aboard.

These Davis rafts were generally between 150 and 250 feet long and were made by weaving a mat of logs, chains and cables; the mat was one-half to one-third as wide as it was long. Then loose logs were piled on top until the mat was 6 to 8 feet under water. More cables and chains were wrapped around the whole thing and cinched tight with steam donkeys. These rafts carried up to a million board feet. In later years, 500-foot-long Davis rafts were built; they drew 24 to 25 feet of water and carried 2.5 million feet.

A great advantage of the Davis raft was that it could be towed in much rougher weather than a flat boom, even in the ocean swells of the west coast or across Hecate Strait. The enormous demand for airplane spruce during World War I made the Davis raft a much-used towing technique. In the Charlottes, a number of rafting centres were established. Bags and, occasionally, flat booms were towed in and rafting crews made up the rafts. The first raft to be towed out of the Charlottes across Hecate was in 1917 by Capt. Alfred Lewis on the *Progressive*.

A much larger, more powerful tug could be used on these rafts than on the flat booms, so the big old ship-towing tugs like the *Lorne* were again in demand. The procedure for towing rafts was a little different from towing booms. When the weather was good, a

43

Doug Stone
Former president, Stone Bros.

The first diesel-engine tug in Alberni Canal was a boat called the *Port Alberni*, owned by Captain Sid Croll. It was a six-cylinder Washington. It wouldn't start one winter, so he tried to prime it with gasoline and had an explosion that bent the crankshaft and ruined the engine. The Washington people replaced it free of charge. I don't know how he talked them into it, but they put a heavy-duty four-cylinder Washington in the boat and it ran for years and years. As a matter of fact, I believe it's still running.

I can remember my dad saying, "We'll have to watch out for that boat or we'll not have any towing left. We'll have to get cracking on converting." I think this was about 1926 or 1927.

Nobody liked the diesels then; they were too noisy and smelled bad. With the steamers there was no noise, except a faint click here and there if something was loose, and you'd hear the propeller going around. They were marvelous things, those steam engines. If only they had a better combustion system and a better boiler system they would have been dandy, but they took up so darn much room and the fuel took up the rest of the room so there wasn't any room for much else.

boat like the *Lorne* would take advantage of it and tow raft after raft across Hecate Strait; each trip might take as long as two days. The tugs would tie up the rafts at various points along the inside passage. Then, when the weather got too rough to tow across Hecate, the tugs would pull the rafts down the coast, sometimes taking them all the way, often tying them up where they would be picked up by other tugs and moved a little farther south. An entirely new phase of towboating was under way.

44. The *Point Garry* on the ways being repaired in 1919; owned by B.C. Department of Public Works. The 50-foot tug or motor-dredge tender was built in Victoria and had a 55-horsepower Imperial engine.

5 / The Golden Age of Towboating

The decade of the 1920s was one of unprecedented prosperity on the B.C. coast and, in many respects, can be looked upon as the golden age of towboating.

Prior to 1920, most industrial activity in the province had been centred on the south end of the Strait of Georgia and Vancouver Island. Very little logging had been done north of Queen Charlotte Sound, the up-coast mining camps had been self-contained, and fishermen had been contracted to work for particular canneries and had confined their fishing to specified areas.

After 1920, however, this pattern of resource development was drastically altered in scope and character. The strong demand for lumber and the experience gained in towing logs out of the Queen Charlotte Islands during the war opened up the entire coast to logging. The invention and widespread use of internal combustion marine engines led to the building of smaller boats which were easier to run and required smaller crews of about seven members. It was even possible to have one- or two-man tugs. This development encouraged hundreds of independent fishermen and towboat operators to go into business for themselves. Fishermen began to work the entire coast, rather than just one inlet or estuary.

An important though short-lived fishing venture was launched in the mid-1920s on the west coast of Vancouver Island. It lasted for only three or four years, the length of time that a large run of pilchards, a small herringlike fish, appeared in those waters. Tugboats became an essential component in this fishery, since they were needed to tow the scows that collected the

45. The *Tartar* in 1921 when she was owned by Coastwise Steamship and Barge, the B.C. arm of James Griffiths & Sons of Seattle.

Mickey Balatti

Retired towboat captain

I was born in Ladysmith on Vancouver Island in 1905 and worked in logging camps greasing skids for the horses to haul logs on. I was a whistle punk in the woods and helped set chokers. I worked in a coal mine in Lantzville. Then in 1924 I came to Vancouver and started working on the steam tugs.

I started out on the old *Brunette* as deck hand on the day after New Year's. She was coaling up in False Creek when I boarded her. It was a very cold winter and False Creek was frozen up, so we had to break the ice out to the boom and then break the boom loose with peaveys.

On the *Brunette* were a captain and mate, chief engineer and second, a cook and a deck hand—six men. The engineer and the second engineer had to fire coal on their own watch; there were no firemen. The deck hand's job was to pass the coal and heave the ashes, and also to work with the mate on the boom. When you weren't working coupling up the booms, you were forever painting or washing paint. It was a kind of pride with the mate on those tugs to have her good-looking. Every time that tug was due to come into Vancouver, you had to have all the brass polished. It didn't matter if it was the wintertime, cold as hell and freezing. You still had to get out and polish that brass.

I remember one time coming into Vancouver, I think I was decking on the *Dauntless*, and washing paint in the cold. After you put the soapy water on, it would turn to ice before you could wipe it off. And you couldn't put too much on because it would drop on deck and leave white marks. When I told the mate it was too cold to polish brass, he said, "Well, boy, if you don't want to do it, have your bags packed and we'll get somebody else." But he was a good mate, a nice guy; if he didn't have the boat all cleaned up, the skipper would be on his tail.

There was no overtime or anything on the tugs. You got sixty dollars a month and board, and they could work you anytime they wanted. They could call you on your off watch.

46. The *C & S* (McKenzie Barge), an early gasoline-powered tug built in New Westminster in 1924 and later renamed the *Margaret McKenzie*.

Sparkie New
Retired president, Coastal Towing

The first time I went to the west coast I went out there for my old pal George Ellis. I took the *Wasp* out, a harbour tug. She was thirty feet long and had a gas engine in her. This was in 1928.

George had got a charter for this boat to tow pilchard scows. On those little tugs it was a one-man deal. Occasionally you might have a deck hand, but most times you didn't.

On that first occasion I was taking the fish scow with me and I had a deck hand. He was an Austrian who couldn't speak much English and got seasick before we got past Point Atkinson.

We headed around Cape Scott and down to Kyuquot. We arrived in Kyuquot fine and dandy— much the worse for sleep as far as I was concerned. The deck hand spent most of the voyage clapping his face on the floor, seasick. So it was quite a voyage. But, you know, we didn't regard it as anything unusual in those days. That's the way things were done and you either made it or you didn't.

Most times you made it. While I was at the plant there, my job was to take one of these fish scows and follow the seiners outside and get the scow loaded and then bring it in to the plant. Entirely alone, no deck hand. This wasn't just a one-day deal. You might drift around for a few hours and get a little sleep. And then away you go again.

They were fishing anywhere up to thirty miles offshore, where they wouldn't be so likely to hit the rocks. Just keeping to seaward, nowhere near the beach where you could really get in trouble.

If you're working with the sea you'd better do what you're able to do with the equipment that you've got. And you're supposed to know what it is you're driving, if you want to live very long.

pilchards from the seine boats which were fifty to sixty miles offshore at the fishing grounds. The business generated by this fishery provided a good start for many people who were to become prominent in the towboat industry.

One of the first towboaters to get contracts for towing the pilchard scows was George Ellis of Vancouver, who operated Harbour Towing. At that time a number of the young, independent towboat operators who had small, one- or two-man boats worked through Harbour Towing; they paid Ellis a small percentage of their income for the use of the office, dispatching and similar services. O.H. "Sparkie" New, who at the time worked for Ellis, later started his own company, Coastal Towing. Another independent was Bill Dolmage.

At the age of nineteen, Bill Dolmage raised some money, got his mother to sign a bank loan and built the *Wee Giant*, a 32-foot tug with a 36-horsepower diesel engine. Through George Ellis, Dolmage won a contract to tow pilchard scows and spent the next four years working off the west coast, usually single-handed. Most towboaters, looking back, acknowledge that this undertaking required almost superhuman stamina, courage and skill. At the time there were some who thought it was utter folly.

While he was towing scows off the west coast, Bill Dolmage met four brothers who were engaged in a similar operation, except that the boat they used to tow their scows into their reduction plant at Matilda Creek was less seaworthy than his. The Gibson brothers were also learning to tow in that part of the coast; since they were about the same age as Dolmage, they all became good friends and shared ideas on improving log-towing techniques.

When Harbour Towing went bankrupt a few years later, Dolmage took it over and operated it under the same name until after the war. Thirty years later, it was the largest log-towing company in B.C. About 1948, the company name was changed to Dolmage Towing.

During the same period, the Gibsons acquired large timber holdings on the west coast of Vancouver Island, built the Tahsis sawmill and pioneered new log-towing and barging techniques—all the result of their willingness and ability to work in an area of the coast that most others avoided.

The Gibsons were involved in some of the earliest attempts to barge logs. Just who was the first person to put into practice the idea of loading logs onto or into another craft is a matter of some dispute. In the early 1920s, Barney Johnson's Hecate Strait Towing converted the hull of the old sailing ship *Drumrock* to a barge and rigged her with loading derricks. In 1925 the wooden-hulled *Bingamon* was converted to a barge by Capt. W. Wingate and put to work hauling out of the Charlottes. In the late 1920s the Gibsons chartered the *Lorne* for a year and, with Harold Hansen as skipper and Drydie Jones as mate, used her to tow the log-laden hull of the *Black Wolf*.

Being a small-scale "gyppo" or independent operation, the Gibsons found Davis rafts too expensive to operate. Not only did Davis rafts require many thousands of dollars worth of cables and chains but they also took a long time to dismantle when they reached their destination—and there was the added expense of shipping the cables and chains back. So the Gibsons devised a new type of raft. Theirs used two mats, which were only half as wide as the mat on a Davis raft. After the logs were loaded on and the cables were cinched up, the two mats were slid out from underneath each side of the raft. The mats were kept and used again, while the raft was towed away. Once the Gibson raft reached its destination, taking it apart was a simple process, and fast. The raft was tied about with ropes, which were then soaked in diesel fuel. The clamps holding the cables tight were removed, the strain being taken by the ropes. The ropes were set on fire, and everyone ran. When the ropes burned through, the raft burst apart and the logs floated free.

Until World War I, most B.C. export lumber had been marketed by American dealers, the majority of them from San Francisco. This dependence on American dealers meant that when markets were depressed, the mills in B.C. were the first to lose orders. At the end of the war, two marketing agencies were set up to improve this situation: a co-operative venture by a number of mills called Seaboard Lumber Sales Company Limited and an independent agency called H.R. MacMillan Export, organized by H.R. MacMillan. At the same time, the federal government established the Canadian Merchant Marine and built twenty freighters; these were leased to private com-

Bill Dolmage

Former president, Dolmage Towing; retired manager, Kingcome Navigation

I met the Gibson brothers in 1925, the first year I was on the pilchards. I went down to their sawmill. Well, you never saw such a collection of junk in your life. The boys were all around my age—Gordon and I are very close, Clarke is older, then Earson, and Jack is the youngest.

I had a little scow with me and the fishing company I worked for ordered some decking to rebuild an old mine dock they had. The planks were supposed to be three-by-twelves but went anywhere from, say, an inch, inch and a half at one end to four inches at the other. There wasn't one plank that was the same thickness at both ends. When we laid it down you couldn't wheel a hand truck over it.

The Gibsons had a little seine boat called the *Anchorite*, with a twenty-horsepower Corliss gas engine, and they went fishing. I don't think Gordon had ever run a seine boat in his life. He was skipper and was up on top of this boat, and she was so small that if he walked over to the side she listed over with his weight on top of the wheelhouse.

She leaked so badly that Earson—that was the third brother—was on the pump all the time, the old fisherman's hand pump. Any time you went by the *Anchorite*, there was Earson on the pump. I think he pumped all day long. No wonder his back gave out.

Clarke ran a little bit of a tender with a two-cylinder twenty-horsepower Deutz diesel engine on it. The little wheelhouse was just off the foredeck, about that high, and he'd have his great head sticking out there. She'd be a little pinnace called the *Gibson Girl* and she was a tender towing a scow for the *Anchorite*.

panies to ship B.C. lumber to the large markets in Australia, South Africa and the Orient.

Although most industrial activity in North America experienced a slight depression after World War I, the lumber business remained strong and continued to expand. The B.C. mills received an additional measure of this wealth because they now had control over the marketing and shipping of their products.

The big lumber companies had large amounts of logs to be towed, so the established towing companies flourished. The hundreds of small, independent loggers who had gone into business a decade or two earlier were also thriving: each of them had logs to be towed and supplies to be hauled.

Log towing, by this point, had developed well beyond the stage of simply tying on a boom and yarding it down to Vancouver. The pattern that developed in the "jungle country" north of the Yuculta Rapids and the Seymour Narrows, such as the area around Minstrel Island, was for smaller tugs to locate there and serve the scores of logging operations which ranged from single-family handlogging operations to 400-man camps.

Once logs are in the water, loggers traditionally prefer to have nothing more to do with them. So the tug crews came in and, in many cases, boomed the logs. Or they might gather together many small one-, two- or three-section booms from a couple of dozen

47. On board the log barge *Black Wolf* at Port Clement on Masset Inlet, in the 1920s. The men raising anchor include Drydie Jones (*2nd from r.*) and Capt. Harold Hansen (*2nd from l.*).

handloggers, each shipping out half a year's production. The tugs would bring these sections together at Minstrel Island, Port Harvey, Simoon Sound or any one of the dozens of bays or protected channels. Then a larger tug like the *Sea Lion* or the *Native* would come up from Vancouver to take the tow, which by this time might consist of fifty or sixty sections, down to Howe Sound or perhaps as far as Vancouver or the Fraser River.

This towing job could take anything from a week to a month, even longer, depending on the weather. If it started to blow southeast, which was highly likely from October to April, the boats would get only as far as Ragged Islands, where they would tie up. While the

boats were waiting for the wind to abate enough to risk taking out the boom, they would probably make a run across the Strait of Georgia to Union Bay and fill up with coal. There were no radios until 1923 when stations were set up at Cape Lazo and Merry Island, so the Union Steamship crews kept track of where the tugs were and sometimes, for a small fee, kept the owners informed.

The huge volume of logs flowing down the coast was headed for sawmills located in Burrard Inlet, False Creek and the Fraser River. The mills required a large inventory of logs in order to maintain a steady operation, to meet special orders and to carry them through the winter shutdown of logging camps. Until the 1920s,

47

48

48. The *Cloe* at the Brooks-Scanlon-O'Brien logging camp at Stillwater, 1926.

49. The booming grounds of the Brooks-Scanlon-
O'Brien logging camp at Stillwater, 1924.

logs were stored on the Fraser and in Burrard Inlet, near the mills. Eventually the high cost of harbour fees and the need for greater storage capacity forced the mills to look elsewhere.

At this point, towboat companies began to acquire their own storage areas in Howe Sound and the North Arm of the Fraser. A towboat company that could not provide a storage area for logs was at a competitive disadvantage when looking for business from the logging companies. With the acquisition of storage areas, towboat companies became involved in the business of breaking up booms and sorting and redirecting logs. Pacific Coyle located at Centre Bay in Howe Sound, Preston-Mann at West Bay, and Young and Gore and

50

51

50. A sawmill on Burrard Inlet in 1928, with its supply of logs in booms and empty lumber barges belonging to Kingcome Navigation.

51. The *G.H. French* was built for G.H. French in 1925 and sold to Pacific Coyle Navigation in 1926.

52

M.R. Cliff set up together at Long Bay. By the mid-1920s these four companies, along with Kingcome Navigation and Canadian Tug, were the busiest log towers on the coast.

The formation of Pacific Coyle Navigation in 1926 marked the first significant merger in the industry. The purpose of the merger was to lower overheads and expand business by bringing together companies whose equipment was complementary. The key figure was E.J. Coyle, who had been in the towboat business for twenty years, first with Greer and Coyle Towing, then alone as Coyle Towing. At the time of the merger, Coyle Towing was the largest on the coast with fourteen tugs; it was also the longest-established company in-

53

52. The *Queen* (Coyle Towing) breaking through ice circa 1924. The 85-foot, 115-ton tug was built in 1914 at New Westminster.

53. The Gore Avenue wharf in Vancouver, 1926. Tugs include the *Pacific Monarch*, the *Earl* and the *Moresby*.

volved in the deal. The three other companies involved were much younger and smaller, though certainly not lacking in experience or good boats. Pacific Tug and Barge, organized in 1922 by H.J. Turney and J.M. Lindsay, brought in five tugs—the *Pacific Monarch,* the *Pacific Imp*, the *Pacific Foam*, the *Earl* and the *McL*—and nine scows. Barney Johnson's Hecate Strait Towing, which had also been set up in the early twenties, owned the *Lorne* and the *Cape Scott* plus three of the earliest log barges, and had helped to pioneer raft and barge towing out of the Charlottes. In 1925, the *Lorne* had set a record by towing a Davis raft of one million board feet across Hecate Strait in fifteen hours. The British Pacific Barge Company, established only a year before the merger, consisted of ten log barges, all converted wooden steamer hulls.

The total assets of the new company were about $1,570,000 and its estimated earnings were $196,000 a year. Coyle was the managing director and Turney, Johnson and Lindsay were all directors. Johnson later took over as managing director. The merger gave Pacific Coyle Navigation a fleet of twenty-one tugs, thirteen barges and nine scows. It was the largest and best-equipped fleet on the coast and naturally came to dominate the industry. More than thirty years passed before another merger of this magnitude occurred.

The use of barges as a form of marine transportation was expanding in several directions. With the

54

54. The *C.N. No. 2* with a railcar barge at Port Mann circa 1930. She was built in England as the *St. Catherines* and bought by the CNR.

conversion of most industries from steam to internal combustion engines, the market for coal gradually declined. However, the demand for petroleum products soon took its place. The oil companies built special barges to carry diesel fuel, gasoline, heating oil, kerosene and naptha for lights, and lubricating oils. Contracts to tow these barges were eagerly sought, since they provided a steady, sure business. Many companies were put on their financial feet by obtaining one.

One of the more inventive towboaters around this time was Claude Thicke, who had incorporated Blue Band Navigation in 1921. Like most towboaters he had a few barges, but he was not content merely to go after the available business. He did a lot of research, came up with some interesting figures and persuaded the Powell River Company that it could save money by burning sawmill waste instead of oil in its boilers. This waste was called hog fuel, owing to the odd sound made by the mill machine used to cut up the slabs and chunks of waste wood into small pieces suitable for burning. What Thicke was after, and got, was a contract to barge hog fuel regularly from Vancouver to Powell River. He put the *Coutli* on that job, and for years she ran back and forth off the Sechelt Peninsula, towing a couple of hog fuel barges at a time. This type of contract developed into a lucrative business for many towing companies.

Throughout the Gulf Islands, barging was the

55. The *Annacis* and her crew at a coal dock in Vancouver, 1925. The 65-foot, 56-ton steam tug was built by Johnson Bros. at Annacis Island in 1909.

chief means of transporting the vast array of products required by the growing communities that had been established there: food supplies, building materials, livestock, feed and machinery. During the 1920s most of this business was handled by Bill Higgs's Gulf Island Transportation Company operating out of Sydney on Vancouver Island. In the 1930s, Higgs moved the company to Nanaimo and renamed it the Nanaimo Towing Company; he also ran the ferry service to Newcastle and Gabriola islands, as well as the North American Towing and Salvage Company, which performed most of the salvage work in the Strait of Georgia. Archie McGillis started a barge service in the Strait of Georgia between Vancouver, Courtenay and Powell River. Appropriately, it was called the Vancouver-Courtenay Transportation Company. In 1929 it was taken over by George Lindsay, who renamed it the Vancouver Barge Transportation Company.

In 1925, Harold Jones and his sister Ruth started the Vancouver Tug Boat Company with the *Atta Boy* (later renamed the *La Fille*), 100-b.h.p. diesel, and launched in 1928 the fine-lined, deep-hulled, 75-foot *La Reine,* 275-b.h.p. diesel. The master's cabin was the only one on deck, with accommodations for the crew below, but there were separate cabins for all, each with hot and cold water. From the day that Arthur Lindsay joined the company as general manager in 1928, Vancouver Tug had a very definite operating policy. He thought that the company should try to specialize and get long-term contracts. At the start of the Depression in 1930 there were too many log towers, so the obvious answer was to specialize in towing barges, or scows as they were called then. In 1932, Vancouver Tug made a contract with Norman English, receiver for the bankrupt forest firm of Wood and English, to barge pulpwood chips from its mill at Englewood, near Alert Bay on Vancouver Island, to the new Crown Zellerbach pulp mill at Port Townsend, Washington—a distance of 250 miles. This contract lasted three years, and was the making of Vancouver Tug; the company never looked back. In the succeeding years, the firm specialized in the transportation of pulpwood chips, hog fuel, newsprint, pulp, limerock, petroleum products, salt and lumber.

In 1925, Harold Elworthy of Victoria left his job with B.C. Salvage, bought a tug called the *Quinitsa*,

renamed it the *Island Planet* and founded the Island Tug & Barge Company. The next year he bought out the Gardner family's small towing operation. Elworthy concentrated on barge work and did very little log towing. Also on Vancouver Island, at Port Alberni, the Stone brothers, who had been running a freight and passenger service in the Alberni Canal, moved into towboating when they built the tug *Victory VI* and started towing barges as well as a few log booms.

By now the towboat industry had acquired a status and legitimacy of its own and was no longer merely an adjunct of another industry. It had also been long since recognized that owning a towboat was not in the same class as owning and operating a dump truck or a bulldozer. The B.C. Towboat Owners' Association was formed around 1920, but it was a somewhat ineffectual organization having no very clear purpose. In 1925, however, the association affiliated with the newly created Vancouver Merchants' Exchange, which brought together all the industries connected with the waterfront. The exchange served as an informal but effective means of co-ordinating the activities of its members. The secretary of the exchange acted as secretary of the various member associations.

The BCTOA's membership grew quickly after 1925 and reached a high of fifty-two towing firms, which included nearly all the important ones. Claude Thicke was president of the association in 1925.

The stepped-up activity of the BCTOA had several far-reaching ramifications, in addition to enhancing the status of towboaters on the maritime scene. One of these was the creation of a new definition of the term

56. The *Prosperative* with a lumber scow in tow in 1926 when she was owned by Blue Band Navigation.

57. The *Pronative* on the ways being repaired, Vancouver harbour, 1925.

"independent": an independent towboater was not a member of the association. This factor became significant when the association issued a rate book listing the prices charged for various jobs. The obvious way for an independent operator to get started was to undercut these prices. The situation was not really a clear-cut case of an oligopolistic industry making exorbitant profits and conniving to exclude the individualistic free enterpriser. Self-interest was obviously present; on the other hand, some independent operators ran worn-out, unsafe boats or were not too concerned about paying their crews.

For many years, members of the association had an informal understanding that they would not undercut

58

59

58. The *Goblin* (Gulf of Georgia Towing) with a Davis raft circa 1930.

59. The 55-foot *Goblin* was built for Gulf of Georgia Towing in 1925.

the rate book prices. The rate book, though not a hard and fast pricing structure, was a guide that prevailed until the 1950s, when the Anti-Combines Act was brought to bear on the industry.

The new status and power of the association was evident when it began to represent the owners in contract negotiations with the Canadian Merchant Service Guild. A Vancouver chapter of the guild had been organized in 1917 to represent masters, mates and pilots. Although the association negotiated on behalf of the owners, the negotiators of the contracts or agreements came from the management of individual companies and, in most cases, they were people who had come up through the ranks or had themselves

Mickey Balatti
Retired towboat captain

There was no radar in those days. You'd have it pretty rough sometimes on those tugs, towing barges on the west coast of Vancouver Island. I was mate on the *Pacific Monarch* with old Dick Jones and we were towing barges out of Nootka Sound for the Gibsons. They were at Tahsis, but had a logging camp just outside of Nootka cannery, on the islands there. They had a skyline between the two islands, and we'd put the barge under the skyline and they'd load the barge with logs that way.

You'd be coming in to pick up at Nootka in a southeaster—we used to call them black southeasters because it was a kind of misty rain, the wind howling and visibility down to about two miles. When the southeaster was blowing hard, you'd be setting in about three knots towards the shore, so you had to counteract the tide and the wind and the current.

It might be getting just about dusk as you made the entrance to Nootka and it wasn't safe to come in because of visibility. Rocks on both sides. So we'd turn around, head her out for sea, steam around all night and then come back in daylight and try to pick it up. But after bucking into that southeaster all night, you didn't know if you were holding your own or going astern or what. So you'd have to come back in and pick up a landfall and figure out where in the devil you were.

Lloyd Sias
Former towboat captain;
master, Port McNeil-Alert Bay ferry

I towed from the north coast. We used to tow Oregon dog booms out of Stewart and take them all the way down to Howe Sound. The Oregon dog booms had a one-inch line with screw-in type dogs. You used an air hammer to put them in and, if you were lucky, you had an air gun to take them out. If not, you had to turn them out by hand and that was quite a chore. Dolmage Towing had a setup at Twin Creeks that was built for taking them down. We'd take out the Oregon dogs and all this enormous gear and sort the logs. The sorted booms went out to their destinations from there.

Out of Ocean Falls we used to get bundle booms. The bundles were enormous, so there were only three to a section, and those sections were big, about ninety-odd feet wide. I remember once we tried to take them up the North Arm of the Fraser and we couldn't get them through the bridges, so we had to take them back and go up the main river.

Weather, tides and crossing Queen Charlotte Sound were quite a problem, but it was a case of going when the weather was good. We did a sort of shuttle service across the sound and tied the booms up at Finn Bay, Smith Inlet, Rivers Inlet or wherever we could find good shelter.

The few of us who worked up here steady worked out of Minstrel Island. We used to go out into the jungles, as we called it, and yard the stuff from places like Sullivan Bay to make up the tows for the big boats. We'd yard the stuff together around Cutter Creek, although Coyle, Cliff and Kingcome used the creek, too. We used a small boat with a three- or four-man crew to do the yarding out of the camps, and made up our own tows. If we had no yarding to do out of the camps, we concentrated on moving the stuff down closer to Howe Sound.

Then the big tugs would come up from Vancouver and start making up their own tows, picking some up here and there until they had a full boom, and off they went.

worked on the boats. In short, everyone at the bargaining table knew what he was talking about and was in a position to make decisions then and there.

In 1930, however, with the Depression breathing down everyone's neck, this bargaining procedure broke down and the guild went out on a bitter strike lasting six months. Much of the rancour that arose was owing to the fact that many of the companies convinced their masters and mates to scab during the strike. It was not difficult to persuade them to work, since jobs were scarce during the Depression. The guild expelled those of its members who worked during the strike. When an accord was finally reached, the guild would not readmit the expelled men, who were unable to work when the strike ended. The companies did not back them because they had to accept the guild's decision as part of the strike settlement.

Mickey Balatti
Retired towboat captain

When I was towing barges to Nanaimo, Ladysmith and Nanoose Bay years ago, those great big railway barges, I came up three or four times against a westerly wind of about seventy miles an hour. That old *Pacific Monarch* was deep—sixteen-and-a-half-foot draft—and she'd keep moving, but I'd have to go way up above Sechelt 'cause the boxcars would roll on the barge. One wheel would lift up off the track, the flange on the other side would fall just inside the track, and you'd have the boxcars off the tracks. But if I whipped the barge around quick, they wouldn't have a chance to roll.

On a lot of these trips to Vancouver Island there would be meat all hung from the ceilings of the boxcars, and it would be swaying, so you'd have to keep heading into the wind.

If it was a southeaster you'd stick her nose into it and go into Porlier Pass and keep her that way. The worst part of the southeasterly was just at the last minute when you got down to the pass—you had to line the lights up to come through it. When you lined the lights up you put her beam onto the sea and just hoped that she'd take three or four good rolls and then be out of it. If you didn't have that timed right, it was very easy to roll the cars off the tracks. I only had one accident. It was a big southeaster, and I guess when we lined the lights up, she took two or three big heaves and rolled three cars off the tracks. We had to bring them back to Vancouver and right them with the big CPR crane.

Bill Sankey
Former secretary,
Vancouver Merchants' Exchange

In the old days, when the B.C. Towboat Owners' Association used to negotiate their labour problems—and I'm going back now to the thirties, the forties—they used to sit down across the table from the union. The union used to be represented at labour meetings by their own labour man and he would have with him a couple of engineers and a couple of masters off the tugs. The owners sat down across from them and they would be the owners themselves—the Lloyd Gores, the Arthur Lindsays and so on.

Neither one would bullshit the other. They were both fully aware of what everyone else did because a lot of the owners had come up through the ranks themselves.

I think they went thirty years without a strike, a long time. They always worked out something amicably—give a penny, take a penny.

60. The *Victory VI* (Stone Bros.) was built in 1927 and had a 36-b.h.p., four-cylinder Thorneycroft Petrol/Perofine engine.

61. The *La Reine* (Vancouver Tug Boat) in Coal Harbour, Vancouver. The tug was built in 1924 and retired in 1964.

6 / Half-Speed: The Depression and War Years

The stock market crash of 1929 had an immediate and catastrophic effect on coastal resource industry in British Columbia. Logging and lumber production that year had been the highest on record, but within a year both the export and domestic markets all but disappeared. The United States Congress quickly imposed an import duty of four dollars per thousand board feet, cutting B.C. exports to that market. Shortly afterward, Britain dropped her free trade policy, imposing a ten per cent tariff on imports, and British lumber importers turned en masse to lower-priced Russian suppliers. At the same time, lumber markets slumped in Australia, the Orient and South Africa.

The fishing industry was also hard hit. The international financial upheavals that occurred at the end of 1929 seriously disrupted sales of that year's catch. Then, in 1930, taking advantage of exceptionally large salmon runs, the canneries packed a near-record two million cases, most of which they were unable to sell. The mining industry was crippled by falling metal prices. Falling grain prices reduced the flow of grain through Vancouver by 17.5 million bushels, drastically curtailing shipping.

In spite of all these difficulties, many sectors of the coastal economy proved to be surprisingly resilient. Acting through Seaboard Lumber Sales and H.R. MacMillan Export, B.C. sawmills were able to negotiate large lumber sales with Britain, and by 1938 almost half the timber cut in the province was going there.

The Depression caused the most hardship in cities such as Vancouver and Victoria, where survival was dependent on the prosperity of industries which, in

62

62. The *M.T. Co. No. 1* tied alongside a scow loaded with lumber, 1933. The letters in the tug's name may stand for Marpole Towing.

63. On 19 September 1930 the hulk of the *Pacific Gatherer* in tow of the *Lorne* struck a span of the Second Narrows Bridge. The bridge was not rebuilt until 1934, so cars were ferried across Burrard Inlet eighteen at a time, causing long delays.

64. The *Victory IX* (Stone Bros.) moving out Alberni-Pacific Lumber's Camp 4 from Underwood Cove, 1937. Doug Stone, Jr., eighteen years old, at the wheel.

65

turn, were dependent on the vagaries of international financing. Before long, more than 18,000 of the province's urban population were unemployed and living in relief camps. The coastal rural population, however, was better fitted to ride out the bad times. A handlogger in Knight Inlet, for instance, could grow and gather food for his family and earn money by cutting timber to meet the needs of the B.C. market. In fact, these small, dispersed operations were far more flexible than the large logging camps, which were forced to shut down when the demand for logs at the mills fell below a certain level.

The economy of the coast was held together during

Ray Bicknell

Retired vice-chairman,
Gulf of Georgia Towing

You'd never buy a line or a pike pole, always find them somewhere. We used to accuse other companies of stealing all our lines. We'd steal everybody's line, too. We'd go alongside a ship with a barge and make them throw a line to tie up the barge. It would be theirs, but if we could get them to throw it off we'd have a line.

Same way with boom chains, everybody was stealing boom chains. We were supposed to return boom chains to loggers, but usually they were all lifted. You'd take a boom of logs into False Creek, intact, and maybe three or four days after somebody would go along and steal most of the chains out of it, and the logs would all be bellying out, losing some.

It was a big game in those days, a tough game, the competition was great. There were a lot of towboat companies, many small ones. Of course, the bigger ones tried to regulate the price, but were unable to do that because the smaller ones would undercut us—competition.

65. Three Pacific Coyle Navigation tugs, the *Coyle No. 1*, the *G.H. French* and the *Jessie Mac* working together to tow log booms circa 1935.

the hard years of the Depression in large part by the towboaters. They were usually independent of external financing, were adaptable in their operations and were able to keep operating at reduced levels. In order to survive, the towboat companies lowered wages, reduced crew sizes so that seven-man boats went out with three or four men, chopped food bills and delayed boat maintenance. An indication of the stability of the towboat industry at this time is that, with the exception of Blue Band Navigation, there were no significant bankruptcies. And in the case of Blue Band, the financial difficulties grew out of one owner's unsuccessful dealings in the stock market, not out of a failure of the company itself.

From its earliest days, the logging end of the forest industry had been dominated by the lumber mills. They owned the big timber leases and could raise the substantial capital required to set up 400-man logging camps and to build logging railways along the coast. In the 1930s, because of a number of factors, some independent loggers, who did not own mills, were able to become established and sell their logs on the open market.

One factor was the inability of the larger logging camps to remain open at reduced levels of operation. Another was the introduction of truck logging, which began in the Fraser Valley around Mission and

66

66. The North Arm jetty sometime in the 1940s or '50s. The jetty protected log booms stored in it from wind and swells; it was the largest freshwater booming ground in Canada.

Bill Dolmage

*Former president, Dolmage Towing;
retired manager, Kingcome Navigation*

I'll never forget this. It was just around Christmas time. We brought down a big tow of balsam from one of George O'Brien's camps, and he sold sixteen sections to Westminster Shook Mills. I sent Tony Cosulich over for it with the *A & L*, and I said to him, "Get that tow over to the river, get it up to the North Arm in the jetty somewhere. Tie it up and then take your holidays for Christmas."

Tony had never yarded a boom at night in his life, but he went up to Centre Bay and yarded out the tow and got over off the North Arm jetty. A westerly came up and he was late on the tide, and there's the whole tow up on the beach.

I was out there. What an experience. The tow was right up in all that rock pile along Point Grey. Oh, a long shallow beach. If you get logs on a pretty steep beach, it isn't too bad, you can back in and not have too far to pull them into the water. But if you can't get near them, it's just awful. And there were boulders to get them over, too.

I got Gordon Horie and his pile driver—this is all part of the towboat cost—but the pile driver didn't work out at all. Then I got hold of Art Kyle, one of the characters of the coast if there ever was one. He was the best derrick man this country's ever known. If Northern Construction had a difficult job, they'd call Art in with his old rig to do the job.

I went up with the old *Ironbark*, towing Art's rig on a barge, and it was blowing a gale, a southeast wind, and a big ebb in the North Arm. I said, "Art, I think we'd better wait until the flood." It was not the time to go down the North Arm, with a big ebb and a southeast wind behind you.

He said, "If you can get your boat down there, don't you worry about me." We got down to Mitchell's Slough and I blew for the bridge and, of course, they were always slow on opening it. I kept going. Just as we were about to enter the span, which was not much wider than the barge, I came up standing. I was going full speed ahead but I wasn't going anywhere.

The old boy had thrown out the clamshell bucket from his derrick, like a great big anchor, and brought everything up standing. So he just eased up on his bucket and we went through that bridge.

We got down off the mouth of the river and started hauling logs.

I had two or three of the river tugs with me there, and we worked till New Year's Eve. I remember sending one of the boats up to Marpole to a bootlegger I knew. I said, "Go up and get a couple of bottles of rum." Because here we were down at the North Arm jetty picking up logs on New Year's Eve.

We were moving the logs around and I was up to my waist working in the water—it was just freezing cold. But you had to do it. There was no insurance and the logger told you straight: you lose my logs, you pick them up.

When Bob Cosulich went up to Prince Rupert to buy the *James Carruthers* for White Rock Tug, he said the grass was growing two feet off her deck. They had tied these trawlers up and never looked after them. The machinery was all rusted—they had to take the steam engine, every part, up to the shop to turn it down in the lathe, and rebush everything.

They had quite a time changing them into towboats. The trouble with a trawler is that the machinery is all aft and the fishhold forward. So there really isn't room on the afterdeck to put a towing winch. What they did on the *Foster* and *Kelly* was to use the big trawl winch, which is a double-drum steam winch right below the wheelhouse on the foredeck, and they ran the towline under the wheelhouse, over the top of the boiler and through the funnel. They put a pipe through the funnel so the towline wouldn't get too hot, I guess. They had big leads aft of the funnel so that no strain could possibly come on the funnel.

On the *Carruthers*, they ran the towline around the funnel in great big shivs so it couldn't possibly straighten out and take the funnel off. When you think about it, it was haywire. Those towing machines were built to pull from forward for trawling. They weren't built to take the strain from the stern like towboating.

I remember that the skipper, Johnny Campbell,

used to worry about this towing machine. He could see it down there in heavy weather working back and forth. If it ever let go, away would go the wheelhouse, the funnel, the whole works. So he used to run wires from one drum of the machine up forward to great big bollards and heave that up tight, then have the towline running out over the stern.

I remember the accommodation on the *Carruthers*. The skipper was up in the wheelhouse, a little bit of a wheelhouse, just enough room for the bunk aft of the wheel. First boat I'd ever seen where there was a compass over the skipper's bunk so he could see what they were steering at all times. The chief engineer, the second engineer and the mate were down aft of the engine room.

When I got her, she had been fishing and had carried a crew of twenty-seven or twenty-eight men. They were all down in the forecastle in bunks, five high, right up to the decks on either side with the galley table down in the middle. No refrigeration.

I changed her around a lot. Put in a huge icebox that carried about seven or eight hundred pounds of ice, so the food was better. I cut up the forecastle so there were only two men to a section—we carried ten men.

I used to charter that boat to the Powell River Company for log towing. She burned eight tons of coal a day which we paid about six dollars and something a ton for—so roughly fifty dollars a day for coal. This was during the winter months when tugs lost many days for weather, saving coal. We got a hundred and ten dollars a day for the boat with ten men on it. And we found that even with the cost of the coal, the wages and the grub, we made money. It's hard to believe.

I think the cook was paid fifty dollars, the skipper, a hundred and sixty; the chief engineer, a hundred and fifty; second engineer, a hundred and a quarter. At that time a crewman got forty-five.

When the war started I knew the *Carruthers* was too much to leave, so when the Gibsons offered to buy it from me I sold it to them. After the war, when I came back, Clarke phoned me and said, "Bill, would you operate the *Carruthers* for us?" They were logging on the west coast at the time and were making up Gibson rafts.

I said, "Clarke, leave that old relic at the dock. She's had her day." The old *Carruthers* was still a coal burner. "You've only got two or three rafts left," I said, "give them to somebody to tow."

But no, they wanted to keep operating the *Carruthers*. I found a skipper in Seattle who had a Canadian ticket. He said he'd take her, but he'd never towed a Davis raft or a Gibson raft in his life. So he came up and away they went.

This skipper said to Gordon, "How much weather will that thing take?" looking at the raft.

Gordon said, "You just head out there and don't look back. Just keep going." That's Gordon's way of doing it—don't look back.

Well, then the Gibsons went into the whaling business. They put a gun on the *Carruthers* and sent her out. When they finally packed up the whaling, the boilers in the *Carruthers* were finished, so they gutted her out as a hulk to carry herring from the Queen Charlotte Islands. I guess her bulkheads were as thin as paper because she foundered in Hecate Strait and down she went full of herring, with nobody on her. That was the end of the *Carruthers*.

Lloyd Sias

Former towboat captain;
master, Port McNeil-Alert Bay ferry

When I worked on the river, we used to have an interesting operation towing out of Sumas. We'd make up our tow; take down the boom numbers and head on down. When we got down just below Silverdale we used to let the tow drift and we'd run ahead down to Whonnock. Go in there, run up to the pay phone, call the office and give them our list of boom numbers.

They'd give us our destinations if they had them. Sometimes they'd have to phone to the brokers or whoever it was who owned the logs to find out where they were going. Then we'd get our orders and we'd be gone.

Lots of times the boom would be drifting down by Albion before we caught up with it again. It just drifted straight on down the river. It was a funny way to do things, but there was no radio telephone.

Harrison, then spread up the coast. Logging trucks could go into the steeper areas where railways could not. Trucks also cost a lot less than locomotives and made it possible for an independent logger to establish a business on a scale more profitable than that of a handlogger.

A third factor was the development of storage and sorting grounds in Howe Sound in the 1920s. Because these grounds were controlled by towing firms, not the mills, a boom belonging to an independent logger could be towed there, broken up, sorted by grade and species, and sold on the open market to the highest bidder. This situation encouraged close working relationships and often friendships between loggers and towboaters.

One of the more prosperous and long-lasting of these relationships was that between Bill Dolmage and George O'Brien, a major independent logger. During this era O'Brien, his pockets full of cash, occasionally went out with Dolmage on one of his boats. They went from one handlogging operation to another, buying up small booms until they had a tow worth taking to town. Sometimes these handloggers were not too excited about the prices offered, but they got hard cash, a scarce commodity on the coast at that time. They were also relieved of the responsibility for paying the towing, insurance and broker's fees, and waiting for the boom to be sold.

In 1936, O'Brien had seven million board feet of cedar that needed towing down from the north coast, but Dolmage did not have a suitable boat to do the job. They discovered that the White Rock Tug Company, which had just become bankrupt, had acquired a North Sea steam trawler, the *James Carruthers,* and converted her to a tug. Dolmage and O'Brien took the *Carruthers* over for $5,200 and set up a company called Northwest Towing. They towed the cedar in three trips, which paid for the boat. For a skipper they hired Johnny Campbell, reputed to be one of the coast's most skilled log towers; he had been working for Pacific Coyle Navigation, which was having financial difficulties. This towing operation firmly established Dolmage in the log-towing end of the business. Twenty years later, when Dolmage was made manager of Kingcome Navigation, by then the towing arm of the newly created MacMillan Bloedel forest company, O'Brien became vice-president in charge of logging.

In the 1930s the last of the sailing ships were being towed into Vancouver harbour. Now completely replaced by steamships, they were coming not to pick up cargoes, but to be stripped down and converted into barges to haul logs from the Queen Charlotte Islands and the west coast of Vancouver Island.

So long as loading wharves were laid parallel to the currents, a steamship could easily dock unaided, using its own power to offset the currents. But the construction of finger wharves, which jutted out into the currents, meant that ships had to dock and depart across the current, a difficult manoeuvre for a 400-foot ship in close quarters. Tugs were necessary to control the ships in these situations. As ships became larger, the need for berthing assistance in Vancouver harbour grew and was met by the Cates fleet of harbour tugs. This quickly became a Cates specialty and, in time, the firm became the major berthing company in the harbour.

New Westminster harbour was a deep-sea port from the time of the end of sail until well after World War II. For many years the ships that came up the river eased into dock by themselves. But when they began calling for tugs to assist them, the job was filled by

67. The *Charles H. Cates II* docking a freighter in 1935. The 36-foot tug had a 50-horsepower Union diesel engine, and was built in 1922 as the *Gorilla*.

Westminster Tug, the successor to Cooper and Smith Towing which had been started by Tom Cooper with the *Shuswap*. Eventually, however, the development of larger ships saw the end of New Westminster as a deep-sea port, though it is now a busier harbour than ever.

A number of owner-operated tugs and small towing outfits came into being around New Westminster and the North Arm of the Fraser during the 1930s and '40s. Harry Bruno, who had started towing in the 1920s with the *Prospect Point* and the *Eagle I*, did a lot of work for Canadian Western Lumber. His son Jack joined the business in 1935. They picked up booms at the mouth of the Fraser from Canadian Western's own tugs and took them up to the mill or on to the storage grounds on the Pitt River. In the late 1930s, Jack worked with Pacific Coyle Navigation to sink two old hulls off the entrance to the North Arm in an unsuccessful attempt to create a breakwater.

William Beckman and his son Amos had been operating the 40-foot *VB* and found that most of the business involved yarding logs at the mills or assisting other tugs through the bridges on the Fraser. Amos built a shorter, shallow-draft boat, the *Tugaway*, specifically for these jobs. She was a 30-foot vessel which had the 30-horsepower Vivian gas engine from the *VB*. This type of river towing operation set a pattern that prevailed for two or three decades. The bigger coastal tugs owned by forest companies or the

68. The *Prospect Point* in 1924. Her engine was converted from a distillate engine to a Wolverine diesel in 1923.

mills brought booms into the mouth of the Fraser, where they were either taken over or assisted up through the bridges by the smaller river tugs. The rest of the time, the river tugs did odd jobs around the mills or elsewhere on the river. One such company, Stradiotti Bros., started towing in the North Arm in 1945.

Log barging entered the realm of high adventure in 1934, when the Gibson brothers bought the *Malahat,* a famous old rum-running, five-masted schooner originally built to haul lumber to Australia. When the Gibsons found her, she was under seizure at Burrard Drydock; they were primarily interested in her engines, twin Bolinders which they needed for their

west coast freighter, the *Otter*. They scraped up $2,500 and bought her. After looking around town a bit they secured a contract with Tom Kelly to haul spruce from the Charlottes. First they needed a captain who was qualified to master a full-rigged sailing ship. They hired John Vosper, who had been the *Malahat*'s previous skipper, although running rum to San Francisco was probably a fairly tame enterprise compared to what the Gibsons had in store for him.

Not bothering with the usual twenty-man crew, two of the Gibsons, Gordon and Earson, plus Vosper and a couple of other men, set out from Vancouver harbour, bound for the Charlottes. As Gordon tells it, they ran on the engines until they reached the north

69. The *Eagle VI* (Bruno Towing), Jack Bruno in the stern, 1941. The tug was eventually sunk in a gale off Ballenas Island.

end of Vancouver Island. By this time everyone had pretty well sobered up, so they raised the sails and headed for the Charlottes. Some weather set in, the visibility dropped and, since they were short on navigating instruments, they were not sure where they were. At one point soundings were taken and the water was found to be not all that deep. Not having a big enough crew to reef the sails, they dropped the anchors. When these grabbed bottom, every sail on the ship blew out, like cannons going off.

Poor Vosper. Not only had these crazy loggers wrecked the sails on the ship, but they were proposing further modifications. The *Malahat*'s hatch was only 20 feet long, and the Gibsons were going to load 40-foot logs. They decided to remove one of the masts, lengthen the hatch to 40 feet and rig a loading boom. Vosper, legally in command, refused. The Gibsons waited until the captain fell asleep, then set to work with a crosscut saw and their fallers' axes. By the time Vosper awoke, they had felled the mast, lengthened the hatch and cleared out superfluous decking. A bit of axe work had sharpened up the end of a fir log, which was fitted into a notch chopped into the base of a mast. This improvised loading boom was operated with a steam donkey set on deck. British Columbia's first self-loading, self-propelled, self-unloading log barge was in business.

Eventually the engines on the *Malahat* were

70. The *James Carruthers* towing the log barge *Malahat* (her engines removed) in 1942. Both tug and barge were owned by Gibson Bros.

removed and she was made into a barge, as were several other sailing hulls which the Gibsons bought and converted. In typical Gibson style they also acquired another boat, the *Maid of Orleans*, built in 1882 in San Francisco. She had been a blackbirder, smuggling illegal black semi-slaves from the Solomon Islands to Australia and South America, then became a rum-runner, and had wound up cod fishing in the Bering Sea and trading in the Arctic. In 1934 she went up on the rocks at Sarah Island and was salvaged by Paul Armour of Prince Rupert. She was sold to cover the salvage claim, always an irresistible situation for the Gibsons. For $5,000 they obtained possession and changed her name to the *Joan G*, after one of the

71. On board the *Malahat* when she was a self-propelled log barge, circa 1940. Gordon Gibson (*2nd from l.*), Capt. Dan Backie (*2nd from r.*, arm raised).

Gibsons' daughters. She hauled dynamite, towed rafts and barges, packed herring and pilchards, and eventually was outfitted with the Bolinders out of the *Malahat*.

By 1937 the log-towing business was picking up sufficiently for Sparkie New and George Ellis to set up Coastal Towing. With $500 cash and a $19,000 mortgage, they commissioned marine architect Robert Allan to design the *Hyak*, which was built at Benson Shipyards. A few months later Ellis pulled out and New took over, serving as both master and engineer on the *Hyak*, while Mrs. New ran the office. New had worked for Ellis in Harbour Towing running harbour tugs and towing pilchard scows. He had also been chief engineer on the Union Steamship Company's *Comox*, and had served as both master and engineer along the Mackenzie River for the Northern Transportation Company. Coastal Towing was primarily a log-towing operation and soon acquired the *Jessie Island No. 7*. Later New bought several more tugs: the *Beatrice*, the *Fearless,* the *Gleeful,* the *Active,* the *St. Clair* and the *Petrel*. A highly successful towing company, Coastal was dogged with bad luck in later years, losing the last three named boats.

George McKeen's towing operation, which had started in New Westminster in the last century, moved to Vancouver and was taken over by George's son, Stan. In 1937, Stan McKeen incorporated the Standard

72. The *J.R. Morgan* aground at Lasqueti in 1935 or 1936. Built in 1892 as the *Bruno*, she was renamed the *Prince Albert*, then the *J.R. Morgan*. She was a rumrunner converted into a steam tug owned by Gibson Bros., and was finally broken up in 1949.

73

72

Sparkie New
Retired president, Coastal Towing

We lost the *St. Clair.* That was on the west coast of Vancouver Island. Stan Bell was the skipper and he was a damn good skipper. In those days we were handling the Standard Oil barge, the big oil scow they had. One of the runs was to Port Renfrew, another was Brentwood, but we never quite knew where we were going. So we used to follow what was, in those days, standard procedure: we'd just clear coastwise and then go wherever it was we had to go. That was acceptable to the authorities, as long as you were within your limits, of course.

That's what we did in this case. We cleared her coastwise and we didn't know when she was cleared where she was going. As it happens, she was going to Port Renfrew. She hadn't any more than got there before it started to breeze up a wind from the southwest, which is pretty dirty in Port Renfrew.

At that point, Stan had a choice whether to stay there and ride it out, or to take off and go to the American side and maybe get some more shelter. So he decided to ride it out, which was a perfectly good decision.

He had his anchor down, of course, but she started to drag the anchor, so he started to use the engines. It got worse and worse and he's using a bit more engine at this point. The sea is getting bigger and eventually the scow—which is trailing behind him on a short towline—she swung around. I guess an extra big swell must have hit him and she probably tripped like that, picked up the bight of the towline in her propeller and that disabled her.

The scow dragged the tug ashore into the shallows and the whole business went right up on the beach.

I was out there the next morning and the only thing that you could see of the wreck was the barge, which was broadside to the beach and absolutely flattened. The tug had completely disintegrated and disappeared, except for the boiler, which was a Yarrow boiler. There it was, standing up in the mud with the steam drums on the top, with no boat around it at all. Just pulverized her. Three men lost their lives in that one.

73. Two ex-rumrunners, the *Joan G* (*l.*) and the *J.R. Morgan*, both owned by Gibson Bros., circa 1945.

Towing Company and added three more boats, the *Standfast,* the *Standby* and the *Knockabout.* And in the same year a third company was launched, Horie and Latimer, which, two years later, merged with the Great West Towing and Salvage Company.

Just before the war, in 1939, two well-known towboaters on the lower Fraser, Bob Cosulich and Harry Burt, formed the Cosulich and Burt Towing Company. Cosulich had worked for White Rock Tug, which towed for the Campbell River Lumber Company's sawmill at White Rock and also towed logs from Seattle to sawmills in Vancouver. It built the *Camrilco* to tow lumber scows, taking her name from first letters in the Campbell River Lumber Company, a major shareholder

in White Rock Tug. White Rock also acquired the *Hustler,* the *Almara* and the *James Carruthers* and chartered the *Master.* When the Campbell River Lumber Company went bankrupt, so did White Rock Tug, and Bob Cosulich, who had a minor share in the towing company, lost everything. He was involved with Bill Dolmage for a while on the *Green Cove,* worked some time for Maritime Towing, then went on his own and built the *Celnor* in 1935, a boat that he is reputed to have run almost single-handed for days at a stretch. He was considered a fine towboater, but short on business luck.

Until the 1930s the upper limit for towing on the Fraser was generally considered to be Harrison River and

74. The Standard Towing Co. fleet docked at the foot of Heatley Avenue in Vancouver, 1937. Tugs include (*l. to r.*): the *Marpole,* the *A & L,* the *Standby,* the *Standfast* and the *Stanpoint.* Other tugs shown are the *Robert Preston* and the *Chemainus.*

Harrison Lake. Some logs had been brought down by stern-wheelers twenty and thirty years before, but it was not a common practice. During the Depression, Bill Dolmage began to tow out of Harrison Lake for Dewey Anderson, a well-known logger of that time, and was also involved with George Peebles in a river tug called the *Green Point*. Around the same time a number of people who lived along the river, mostly Indians who had a long association with the Fraser, started towing up the river from Harrison. Charlie Garner, from one of the islands near Chilliwack, had a little tug called the *Sea Garner*, which he used to move small booms downstream. Sam Prest had the *Blue Otter*, Charlie Merchant from Mission had the *Weaver Lake* and the

74

Bill Dolmage

Former president, Dolmage Towing; retired manager, Kingcome Navigation

We used to have to tow down the Fraser River through those gillnetters. One day I was towing all of Dewey Anderson's equipment up to Salmon River with the old *Sea Ferring*. The river boats used to bring down two scows at a time from Harrison Lake, and I'd usually pick them up and carry on. Going down that river you were blowing your whistle, you were doing everything to dodge these gillnetters. They wouldn't get out of your way, but you didn't want to run over top of them.

Anyhow, Dewey had to get six or eight ninety-foot sticks, four-foot square, for a big span to bridge the river. It was a special trip and they were all ready, I just had to hook on to them and take off. They were dogged and wired together so well that I couldn't possibly lose them; they could go through any weather.

So I started down the river. The *Sea Ferring* used to hike, you know, she had two hundred horsepower. She could travel. I was going down and you couldn't see the logs coming behind, just a bit of water coming over the top. I kept blowing my whistle and going right straight down the river. Here these logs are coming along, going right by the tail end of the nets.

When I got up to Menzies Bay I had to wait for the tide, so I took a look at the sticks. I must have had ten ton of salmon along with the fishnets. Boy, the next time I came down the river, they kept out of my way.

E.C.M., and Ed Keech had the *Sea View,* the *River View* and the *River Mite.*

Working on the river with a tug is very different from working on the coastal waters. Not many people who have coast experience work on the river, though it is common for river men to work on the coast. The only sailing condition common to both the coast and the river is the rapids. Coming down the upper river with a boom of logs is like navigating forty miles of the Yuculta Rapids, except that the river is never quite as predictable. The depth and speed of the water varies with the tide and the season, and the bottom is always shifting and changing as sandbars and islands form and disappear from one year to the next. There are virtually no aids to navigation; the channels change so often that it would be impossible to keep such aids up to date. A depth sounder is useless, since by the time it indicated shallow water, the boat or its tow would already be aground.

The only way to navigate that part of the river is to read the water. This is a fine art that is largely instinct, mixed with a lot of skill and a bit of luck. It entails watching the surface of the water and figuring out from the ripples, eddies and other subtle movements what lies beneath the surface of the muddy water. Whether it is six feet deep and safe, or only four and a certain grounding for the tug or boom, is a judgement that only an experienced river man can make.

75

75. The *Red Fir No. 1* (River Towing) made it possible to tow more quickly down the Fraser River from Yale; not to be confused with an earlier coastal tug called the *Red Fir.*

George Peebles was one of the first to master this art and he convinced Bob Cosulich and Harry Burt that, with the right boat, it would be possible to tow logs from as far up the Fraser as Yale. So they built the first of the Red Fir series of river tugs: the *Red Fir No. 1* was a 35-foot, shallow-draft, diesel-powered boat. Burt soon pulled out of the company, and Bob Cosulich's son Cecil came in. The company name was changed to River Towing in 1941. Soon after, the Cosulichs formed an association with the Silver Skagit logging operation to bring out logs from the reservoir site of the Ross Dam on the Skagit River in Washington. It was impossible to take the logs down the river on the U.S. side, so they were brought into

B.C. down Silver Creek and transported by truck to Hope, where they were boomed and taken down the Fraser and over to Puget Sound. When this operation got under way, Cecil's brother, Norman, also came into the company and the Cosulichs proceeded to open up towing on the upper Fraser. The Cosulichs' luck changed for the better, and today their company, RivTow, runs practically all the boats on the river and a large proportion of those on the coast.

When World War II was declared, the B.C. economy boomed overnight. By this time most of B.C.'s forest industry was located on the coast. The once heavily timbered Kootenays had already been overcut and almost all the major interior mills had shut

76

76. The *St. Faith* (Kingcome Navigation) tied up alongside a Davis raft during World War II. She was later renamed the *S.D. Brooks*, then the *Haida Monarch*.

Lloyd Sias

Former towboat captain;
master, Port McNeil-Alert Bay ferry

I can remember once we came down with a big tow with the *Old Faithful* and the *Harvey W.* We were just below Hatzic when the *Harvey W.* hit a boom-chain toggle and punched a hole in her side.

So the *Old Faithful* stopped the tow and tied it up. They drove the *Harvey W.* full speed up on the beach. They had the pumps going, what pumps we had. The tide was falling, as luck would have it, and the *Old Faithful* came up and put her nose against the *Harvey W.* and rolled her on her side a bit, so the hole was just at the water line.

We didn't have anything except an old apple box, so we took it to pieces. We took a wool blanket and cut it into strips and put on a bunch of grease. We shoved grease and blanket into the hole, put a couple of layers of greased blanket over it, and then nailed the pieces of this apple box over it.

We went over and let the tow go and away we went. We brought our tow down to the Pitt and delivered it. Then we went down to the Star Shipyards and they pulled the *Harvey W.* out and put a proper patch on her.

One thing I'll never forget. This happened before I first knew George Peebles and it was an old story on the Fraser. George had a little boat, I think it was called the *Sky Pilot*, if I remember right. He got a job towing scows for Gilley Bros. Things were tough and George couldn't afford a deck hand.

He was coming into the Gilley Bros. dock, where their office was, and there was a bunch of officials from the company at the dock. To make it look good, George would run out on the bow of the tug and yell and wave. Then he'd shout, "Stupid deck hand!" and run back to handle the controls again. He ran back and forth and put on a big show. All he was doing was trying to cover up for the fact that he couldn't afford a deck hand. He was doing everything.

down during the Depression, so most of the massive amounts of lumber needed for the war effort had to come from coastal logging camps. Airplane spruce was once again in high demand, and exports to Britain were stepped up. As part of the Commonwealth Air Training Plan, nearly a hundred airports were planned across Canada, and all the buildings—hangars, barracks, mess halls and training schools—had to be made almost wholly of wood, because of the wartime steel shortage.

Many tugboats were needed to tow the increased flow of logs to the mills, but wartime shipbuilding efforts were concentrated on transport and fighting ships; no new tugs could be built. As a result, the existing fleet was pushed to its limits.

77. The *Island Commander* (ex-*Andrew Kelly*) tied alongside a lumber barge in Victoria in the 1940s.

When World War II started, Bill Dolmage went overseas and quickly established himself as one of the central figures in salvage work with the North Atlantic fleet. When he left for the war, he disposed of a number of boats. The *James Carruthers* was sold to the Gibson brothers, who used her to tow log barges. The *Sea King*, which he had bought in 1939 as the *Olive M* and refitted with a 400-horsepower Atlas diesel and the towing winches off the old *Czar*, was chartered to the U.S. government during the war then went to Young and Gore in 1944. And the Canadian government took over the *Norwest*, originally the *PRT No. 1*, which Dolmage owned through Northwest Towing. The Harbour Towing Company remained intact and by 1946 was owned by Dolmage, Bill Atwood and Cornelius Burke.

The Gibson brothers received contracts to clear land for airport sites at Prince Rupert, Nanaimo and Tofino, with many tugs and barges involved in hauling gravel for the latter. A few other tugs, like the *Island Commander*, were put into service patrolling in the North Pacific, but otherwise there was little direct contact with the war. Following the shelling of the Estevan Point light station, coastal defences were increased and the area off the west coast of Vancouver Island was declared a war zone, giving tug crew members who went into it an extra dollar a day in danger pay. It was possible for tugs in this area to arm

77

themselves with machine guns, but since that would have made them fair game for enemy ships, very few crews took up the government's offer.

The war years had a rather peculiar effect on the towing industry. Production in the forest industry soared and there was a lot of towing work. Since shipbuilding priorities did not include the building of new tugs, very few new companies were formed. Instead, some well-established companies began to buy up other companies.

In 1942 Harold Elworthy decided to leave his partners in Island Tug & Barge. He moved to Vancouver and with Stan McKeen started Straits Towing by purchasing the ten-tug Preston-Mann Towing Company, combining it with McKeen's Standard Towing. They also bought out Commodore Towing, a company owned jointly by Preston-Mann and Young and Gore.

Within a couple of years, however, the opportunity arose to buy Island Tug & Barge. It was purchased jointly by McKeen, Elworthy and Henry Foss. The introduction of Foss represented an important new element in B.C. towboat circles. He was president of the Foss Launch and Tug Company of Seattle, the biggest and one of the oldest tugboat companies on the Pacific coast. Previously he had been involved with Dolmage in Star Towing, a small B.C. company which owned one boat, the *Almara*, but his involvement in

78. The *Torpedo* in Vancouver harbour, 1942. Her first owner was Deeks-McBride in 1925. She burned and sank off Point Atkinson in 1960.

Island Tug & Barge represented the first significant involvement in B.C. towboating by money from outside the country—or, for that matter, from outside the province.

For a while there was talk of merging Straits Towing with Island Tug & Barge, but McKeen and Elworthy, both strong-willed individuals, could not agree on a number of things, especially who would run the joint company. So in 1947 the partners separated. McKeen took over Straits, Elworthy took the major interest in Island Tug & Barge, and Foss pulled out. Straits immediately bought out Union Towing, whose assets included four tugs and the valuable management skills of Fred Brown, who became a significant share-

holder in Straits. That same year McKeen was appointed to the Canadian Senate, providing the industry with a much-needed voice in Ottawa.

This series of events which centred primarily around McKeen and Elworthy was really the beginning of a process that continued for the next twenty-five to thirty years and led to the consolidation of almost all the towboat companies mentioned so far into two giant corporations.

Meanwhile, at Gulf of Georgia, George Walkem had died and the company was taken over in 1943 by two of his sons-in-law, Stavert Byrn and Ray Bicknell. This was followed by a rapid series of ownership changes in other companies. Marpole Towing and

Mickey Balatti
Retired towboat captain

During the war you couldn't get men. They were all in the army. Towing on the west coast was a tough job then because they put all the lighthouses out and camouflaged them. You'd get out there in the misty rain, then you'd have to swing in a few miles to try and pick up a recognizable landmark.

We had numbers on top of the wheelhouse, a big square with our number on it. The planes were patrolling the west coast and they'd swoop down and read our numbers. That was the only sign of life that you'd see out there besides yourself.

They did put machine guns on some of the tugs working out there, but them machine guns would make you an armed vessel and the enemy submarines had a perfect right to shell you if they wanted to. So I didn't want no bloody machine gun on my boat.

Between Estevan Point and Flattery there was an imaginary line, and when you passed that line you were in the war zone. We got a dollar a day extra for being in the war zone. I was pretty happy to get that extra dollar because our wages were pegged for the duration.

Now the owners made a very bad mistake then. They thought they'd done a hell of a good thing by freezing all the tugboat wages for the duration. But when they went to get their rates up they were told, no, you can't do it. So they were stuck, too.

79. The *Union Jack* was built in 1941 for Union Towing. Straits Towing bought Union Towing and renamed the tug the *Burnaby Straits*.

Gilley Bros. were both incorporated into Coleman and Evans (later Ocean Construction), managed by Rufus Gilley. Northwest Towing, started by Bill Dolmage and George O'Brien when they bought the *James Carruthers*, was taken over by Young and Gore. Then business settled down for a few years until 1949, when Straits Towing took over Nanaimo Towing.

At the end of the war a historic event took place a few miles off Cape Flattery, near the spot where Barney Johnson had been picked up by the *Lorne* in the sailing ship that had brought him to Canada. By the time Barney owned the *Lorne*, he had a teen-aged nephew who, after surviving a bout of polio, had been told by doctors that he would die if he had to work in an

80. Fire at Port Alberni in 1947. The freighter *Samtep* caught fire while loading lumber and was towed out into the harbour by the *Victory VII* (Stone Bros.) to prevent the fire from spreading to land.

office. So Barney put his nephew to work on the *Lorne*, and within three years the youngster had his master's ticket. His name was Drydie Jones. Now, in 1946, Drydie was skipper of the *Island Commander*. To him was given the task of towing out the last working sailing ship to visit British Columbia. The *Pamir* had come in from Australia with a load of copra and was leaving with a 4,000-ton cargo of coal. Drydie towed her out fifteen miles off Cape Flattery and let her go in a full gale. It was a fitting close to one era of towboating, which was now on the verge of a revolutionary transformation in organization and equipment.

80

Drydie Jones
Retired towboat captain

The *Pamir* was from Australia, used to bring a cargo over and take coal back. And we'd have to go out and bring her in. That was in 1946. She was the last sailing ship. Two brothers owned her and used to take turns bringing her over and back. We'd tow them out, too, when they were ready to leave.

The farthest we had to go out for her was seventy-five miles southwest of Cape Flattery, Tatoosh Island, because there was hardly any wind out there and he was stuck. When we got out there it was summertime, about four o'clock in the afternoon.

The skipper on there, he says, "Okay, give us a blast on your whistle when you're ready, and we'll be ready to take your line about twenty-five minutes after you tell us." So I blew the whistle, and, Christ, I never saw guys like them. They were just like wasps going up that rigging. We went right in underneath the bow and gave him a line that he made fast. He had no power on that thing, just a generator for lights. To keep the towline from chafing, he had a big piece of canvas with grease on it.

She was a lovely ship. You could eat your meal right off the deck. The fastest trip she made across from Australia took them eighty-one days. She was fast. One skipper on there I used to know pretty well said, "Drydie, the most we ever did with her on a steady wind was twenty knots."

Once we were taking her out with the old *Island Commander*, doing about twelve knots, you know, running light. We had to let her go, we couldn't keep ahead of her. If we hadn't let go, he'd have piled right on top of me, he was going like hell. He couldn't put up too much sail if it was blowing a real gale, only what he figured his rigging would take.

She's gone now, she went down with all hands.

81. The *Island Commander* towing the *Pamir* out to Cape Flattery on her last trip to British Columbia in 1946.

7 / Postwar Change and Innovation

The British Columbia towboat industry managed to successfully survive a decade and a half of Depression and war. As the postwar economy began to build and develop, the late forties and fifties were marked by innovations in water transportation techniques, as well as by sweeping changes in the towboat and forest industries, whose fortunes were closely related.

Peacetime brought with it greatly increased expectations on the part of owners and managers in the towboat industry. Since towing rates had been frozen throughout the war, profits had not been large, though they were sufficient to sustain the industry. The majority of companies were financially sound. The towboat fleet itself, however, was getting old; virtually no boats had been built during the war because of restrictions on shipbuilding, and few boats had been built in the thirties. The bulk of the fleet, therefore, consisted of boats built in the 1920s and earlier. Although many of these were fine boats, they were not very efficient, being equipped with big slow-speed diesels and requiring seven-man crews. The owners wanted to increase efficiency by retooling their boats and reducing the number of men in a crew.

The towboat crews also had high expectations, since their wages had been cut during the Depression and frozen during the war. They felt that fifteen years of hard work and low wages entitled them to some reward. They resisted the proposed reductions in crew size and pressed for higher wages and more time off. Consequently, union activity in the industry increased significantly. Until this point, only masters and mates had been organized: they were members of the Canadian Merchant Service Guild. The view was that a deck hand was like an apprentice; a good one would obtain his ticket and get a mate's position, thereby qualifying for membership in the guild. The guild had grown up with the industry and was mainly a professional organization whose aim was to maintain high standards of seamanship and uphold the traditional maritime hierarchy. Engineers belonged to the smaller National Association of Marine Engineers. The other crew members—deck hands, cooks, oilers— were not organized or represented until the 1950s, when both the Seafarers International Union and the Canadian Brotherhood of Railway, Transport and General Workers organized locals. With the support of these unions, the majority of crew members, who previously had not had a voice, were able to get increases in pay, fewer working hours and improved working conditions, though they had less success in maintaining the size of crews. Relations between crews and owners were harmonious and remained so for many years; this stability formed a solid base for the transformation both in the structure of and the type of work done by the towboat industry.

Significant changes that would affect the towboat industry were taking place in the forest industry, which provided about eighty per cent of the work of the tugs. The first was concerned with the organizational structure of the forest industry. Until the end of the war, there had been several hundred sawmills supplied by twice as many logging operations, most of them independent of the mills. Then in 1950 the provincial government introduced measures that resulted in most of the mills and the majority of timber rights becoming concentrated in the hands of a few giant corporations, practically all of them controlled from outside the province. These quickly became vertically integrated companies, engaged in logging and the processing and marketing of timber products; many of them employed several thousand workers. These giant forest companies consolidated their logging operations, each using one large camp instead of a number of smaller ones. This meant that larger volumes of logs had to be towed from fewer locations.

The second factor was the shift in emphasis in the forest-based economy from sawmills to pulp mills. Before the war, there had been only five pulp mills in the province, none working at capacity. The war multiplied the demand for pulp products in addition to newsprint, and new uses were found for cellulose in explosives, synthetic fabrics and dressings, wallboard and insulation. The demand for woodfibre increased even more after the war, with thousands of products being made from it. By 1972, there were fourteen pulp or pulp and paper mills on the B.C. coast. This shift in emphasis affected the log transportation requirements of the integrated forest firms. When only five mills had been operating, the largest volume of logs had been towed to sawmills located in the Vancouver area. Then, however, pulp mills were built all over the coast, in Prince Rupert, Kitimat, Campbell River, Gold River, Crofton and Nanaimo, so that the largest volume of logs were no longer moving southward as they had traditionally, but in many directions.

The third factor was that pulp mills could use sawmill wastes as well as smaller lower-quality logs. The fourth factor was that hemlock, which had never been in demand despite its abundance, was now being used for pulp and lumber. This was the result of the Koerner family's pioneering efforts to properly dry and season hemlock to make it an acceptable wood; it was marketed as Alaska pine. Unfortunately, hemlock has a propensity for sinking, making it all too easy to lose hemlock logs from a flat boom.

As a consequence of these basic changes in the forest industry, towboat companies had to devise new techniques for transporting logs in booms and rafts. Bill Dolmage was the first to try bundle booming. Columbia Cellulose had a lot of cedar that it wanted towed

Mickey Balatti
Retired towboat captain

Towing across Hecate Strait, we used to make Prince Rupert our headquarters. We'd have to cross the strait to fuel up and grub up there and we'd cross so that we could have good weather by the time we got over and got hooked up. The weather might have changed and we might have a break to get the rafts across.

One time, it was in the fall, insurance was already off the rafts, but this raft was in really tough shape. The teredos were in it and Powell River wanted to get it down as quick as they could before it was worthless.

"Try it, try it," they said, so I got a good weather report and I started off. I got six miles from Triple Island when the wind came up. It hit a hundred and seventeen miles an hour at Green Island. We had to let the towline go and we were very lucky to get in.

There were six fishermen out there, draggers. One couldn't get his net up quick enough, so we tried to bring him in, but he was right in around the rocks by Triple and the fish boat was making about the same pip on the radar screen as the rocks were. You couldn't distinguish what was rock and what was fish boat.

I got within half a mile with the wind blowing like that, and the tug hard to handle. Told him I'd be back out again if he got into trouble and went up in behind Melville Island.

The weather cleared up and we were icing up pretty badly even when we let the towline go. The davits were building up, you could see them building up, and there was a sheet of ice all over the starboard side. You couldn't open or close a window, but I told someone to open up a port door and keep it open because we didn't want to get frozen in.

Anyway, the logs had been coming out of the raft. The tug would roll, and a log would hit the guard and roll away and come back and hit the tug again. If she hadn't been synchronized like that, the log would have hit the hull and gone right through to the engine room.

The deck hand says, "Any danger, captain?"

"No," I says, "no danger." Because you can't get panicky.

82

83

Alex Rodgers

Retired towboat captain

Log towing is far different from barge towing. I liked the logs much better. It could get monotonous because you're only moving about a mile an hour at times, but I think there's more to it because the tides set you harder, different ways, and you have to watch your weather more. If you do get caught in the tide, it takes a little more of your skill.

But you've got to know what you're doing tying up barges, too. With the old wooden scows you had to watch them for leaking all the time. I've been down in more wooden scows than enough, patching. You'd look down and see a little spurt of water coming up off the bottom of the scow. You figure, well, I'll put a plug in there. So you make a little plug and, as you tap it in, the hole is getting bigger. The teredos are eating the hell out of the wood. You cut the plug off and put a piece of sacking or canvas down, with grease, and then you put a board over it with a brace up to the deck to try to hold it and plug the hole.

To stop the barge from deteriorating, they put salt or something in them and it got mushy, brown and slippery. You'd go down in there and by the time you came out you'd be a mess.

When you were towing, or sometimes even at the dock, the scow would start to go over. They had what they called limbers, spaces under the keelson so that the water would spread evenly over the whole barge, instead of building up on one side. When they worked on the barges in the shipyard, instead of cleaning out all the shavings and wedges, they'd leave them in there. Sometimes this stuff would get across the limbers and prevent the water from going through, so the scow would take a list. You'd be pumping out one side and, all of a sudden, the wedge would wash out and everything would shift to the other side.

We had little one-lunger portable gas pumps, but half the time they wouldn't start or would get plugged up and you had to prime them all the time. On the steamboats we had siphon pumps; they never plugged up and were much faster than the gas pumps. Gas pumps weren't very reliable; they still aren't today.

82. The *La Pointe*, owned by Vancouver Tug Boat, with a loaded chip scow in tow, 1959.

83. The *Davis Straits* (Straits Towing) with an empty barge. John Manly built a second tug by this name in the 1950s.

down from Prince Rupert, but it did not want to go to the expense of barging or of building Davis or Gibson rafts. Dolmage persuaded Columbia to make bundles of thirty to fifty logs, held together with a wire cable. These bundles were then boomed up, like logs in a flat boom. The use of bundle booms quickly spread. The technique was particularly useful in moving a heavy species such as hemlock, because it could be combined in each bundle with a lighter species like cedar to help flotation. Another advantage was the lower cost of construction in comparison with Davis or Gibson rafts. And since bundle booms held together better, withstood rougher seas and had a deeper draft than flat booms, they were better suited to the larger and more

powerful tugs now available.

Pulp mills also created a whole new set of demands for barging. Barging itself was not a new technique; since the birth of the towboat industry, coal, lumber, sand, gravel, machinery and a variety of other materials had been transported by barge. The forest industry, however, had so far moved the bulk of its materials in towed booms or rafts. Now it began to use barges in a wide variety of ways. For instance, the chip supply for many pulp mills was often drawn from sawmills that were a hundred miles or more away; hundreds of barges, first made of wood and later steel, were built to move these sawmill wastes. Chip barges had a second function, serving as floating storage facilities when tied

84. The *Sea Foam I* (Dolmage Towing) weather-bound with a log boom in Westview, 1951. The 50.5-foot tug had a 440-b.h.p. diesel engine and carried a crew of five.

up at the mills. Pulp mills also required large amounts of chlorine for bleaching, so special barges were made to carry it.

The paper mills at Powell River and Port Alberni shipped huge rolls of newsprint which, at first, were loaded into covered barges. However, every time these rolls of newsprint were handled, the likelihood of damage was increased. The solution was to load the rolls into railcars at the mill; then the cars were loaded onto rail barges and unloaded at a railhead, making additional handling of the paper unnecessary.

Towing barges is considerably different from towing log booms. A barge, at times, seems to have a mind of its own; it can take control of the tug with dire consequences for the boat and for those on board. In a high wind, an empty chip barge acts like a good-sized sail and has been known to outrun the tug that is towing it. Or a barge may get caught by the tide and sheer off, flipping its tug over or dragging it under.

Log barges did not supplant log towing, at least in the early stages. Quite the contrary, as is shown by the growth of Dolmage Towing over a ten-year period. When Bill Dolmage returned from overseas he still owned most of Harbour Towing, which worked mainly on the Fraser. Eager to get back into coastal log towing, he was confronted with a shortage of good towboats. There were available, however, a considerable number of U.S. war surplus wooden tugs, which the Americans

were selling off at bargain prices. Dolmage quickly picked up the *P.B. Anderson*, the *Sea Prince*, the *Sea Queen*, the *Sea Lark* and the *Sea Giant*, as well as the *Sea Monarch*, a converted U.S. Coast Guard boat. These vessels, together with a few more acquired along the way, quickly made Dolmage Towing the major log-towing company on the coast. He and his partners, Bill Atwood and Cornelius Burke, also reorganized Harbour Towing into a Fraser River-based operation called Pioneer Towing, which specialized in towing logs out of Harrison Lake and down the Fraser.

These surplus boats were instrumental in helping Dolmage Towing to rise so quickly to its position as preeminent log tower in the early fifties. It was not that there was a lack of competition, because the prewar log-towing companies—M.R. Cliff, Pacific Coyle and Coastal Towing, to name some of the major ones—were still in business. But their boats were getting on in years and, even when repowered, could not compete with the war surplus tugs. And some operations, like M.R. Cliff, were slow to convert their tugs, many of which were still powered with steam. The older tugs also required larger crews, more maintenance and were more expensive to operate. At the same time, the demands being made on the industry were increasing rapidly.

When Harold Elworthy had helped found Island Tug & Barge back in the 1930s, the firm had done very little log towing. But after the war, when he left

85. The M.R. Cliff Tugboat fleet at dock in 1949. Tugs include (*l. to r.*) the *Seaswell*, the *Prospective II*, the *Queen*, the *Haro*, and the *Moresby*. It was a holiday tradition to place a Christmas tree on top of the mast.

86. The *Snohomish* (Island Tug) towing a barge holding six war surplus 75-foot steel tugs from Seattle to Buenos Aires, 1947. The barge was submerged in a floating drydock and the tugs were floated in over it; when the barge was re-floated, the tugs were in place on it.

Stan McKeen and Straits Towing to return and take over Island Tug, he implemented some major changes. The company soon had a fleet of fifteen tugs and ten barges, most of them equipped for hauling logs. One of these boats was the *Snohomish*, a powerful deep-sea tug built on the U.S. east coast in 1908. She was dispatched to Argentina in 1947, towing a barge on which were loaded six U.S. surplus tugs. This extraordinary 10,000-mile tow launched Island Tug into deep-sea towing. In 1954 Elworthy spent $500,000 to buy another deep-sea tug, the 193-foot, 2,750-horsepower *Sudbury*. She was a former British navy corvette, brought to British Columbia by Straits Towing, then sold to Badwater Towing (a subsidiary of

Pacific Mills which owned the Ocean Falls pulp mill).

Within weeks of her purchase, the *Sudbury* and the *Island Sovereign* (a 117-foot, 2,400-horsepower tug) were sent to Venezuela to tow four tankers the 5,000 miles to Victoria. Elworthy converted these tankers into self-dumping log barges, an improvement on the self-unloading barge. The barges were rebuilt so that their holds could be quickly flooded, allowing them to tip over and the logs to slide off into the water. The holds were then pumped out, righting the empty barges. This procedure was a time- and labour-saving improvement over the one used with old sailing ship hulls, which had to be unloaded one log at a time by booms or cranes. The idea had originated with Floyd Kurtz, general

87

88

87. Island Tug & Barge's *Island Sovereign* bringing the CPR's cargo liner *Maplecove* into Strait of Georgia in December 1952.

88. Island Tug's *Island Commander* towed the riverboat *Delta King*, from San Francisco to Kitimat, to serve as a dormitory for workers.

manager of Kingcome Navigation, in the early 1950s. The first two self-dumping barges were built for Kingcome by Burrard Drydock, and were the prototype of the specially built log barges that gradually came into common use.

These log barges required large, powerful tugs capable of towing them safely through the open waters of the west coast of Vancouver Island and the north coast. At this time, Island Tug was one of the few companies adequately equipped with proper tugs for the job. In large part this was because the firm was in the deep-sea salvage business, and barge towing was a convenient and profitable way of utilizing its powerful tugs when they were not on a rescue mission.

The *Sudbury* soon began to establish herself as one of the most capable salvage tugs in the Pacific, if not the world. Deep-sea salvage had always been the preserve of the Dutch, who stationed enormous tugs all over the world. It is a hazardous, risky business, not only because of the dangers involved but also because salvage contracts are normally undertaken on a no-cure, no-fee basis. The necessary combination in this business is a company willing to take risks, the right boat and a good crew. Elworthy was more than willing to take a chance, the *Sudbury* was the right boat and her skipper, Harley Blagborne, was a B.C. master with deep-sea experience.

In November of her first year with Island Tug, the

89

89. The famed salvage tug *Sudbury*, owned by Island Tug & Barge.

90. Close-up view of the *Sudbury*'s massive towing
winch.

91. The *Sudbury* and the *Island Sovereign* towing four empty oil tankers in tandem from Venezuela to Victoria, 1954.

Bill Dolmage

Former president, Dolmage Towing;
retired manager, Kingcome Navigation

Quite often the log barges wouldn't dump their loads if they hadn't been loaded properly. You'd flood the tanks and they'd go over on their side, but the logs would just sit there. I was the first one to put explosives in between the logs on the high side. A dangerous thing to do, when I look back on it. You never knew when that load was going to let go. It would sit there for an hour or two and then, all of a sudden, away she'd go, and lord help anybody who happened to be alongside.

I'd had a lot of experience with explosives during the war, so I knew how to handle it. This boom man who I had in Howe Sound and myself, we'd go along and shove bags in between the logs. We'd put about four or five bags down the side with twenty sticks of powder in each. We had what they called cordex to connect one to the next. Then we got well away, pushed the button, and away it went.

That was some explosion. It used to scare the hell out of everybody.

We did one in Vancouver harbour right in front of the grain elevator over on the North Shore. We should have turned the barge around so the explosion more or less went across the harbour, but we had the barge facing North Vancouver, and close in. Well, all the dust around the elevator just went up like a volcano. I thought for sure we'd blown it up, but I don't remember paying for any damage.

On another occasion in Vancouver harbour, the tug skipper of the *Haida Chieftain* called me and said, "The load won't go." Although the log barge had derricks on her, you couldn't use them with a list like that because it put too much strain on the pedestals.

I went over and there she was, lying right over on her side. So I said to the skipper, "Give me this tug for about two minutes and we'll get that load off."

He said, "What are you going to do?"

I said, "You just step to one side." I went back about a hundred yards, put her half speed ahead, and rammed the end of the logs hanging over the stern of the barge.

Well, those logs came down. Of course, they were ahead of me, so there wasn't a chance of a log coming down on top of us.

After that, they used to do it quite often with the tugs, but they had to be shown once.

Sudbury made what is still considered one of the Pacific's greatest rescue operations when she brought in the *Makedonia* through 3,500 miles of storm-lashed ocean. The Greek freighter had run into trouble northeast of Japan when her propeller came loose. The *Sudbury*, then on a barge run out of Nootka Sound, got a radio message to go to the crippled ship's aid. She tied up her barge in the sound and twelve days later, most of them spent fighting high seas, she reached the *Makedonia*. Attaching a towline, she headed for Adak in the Bering Sea, where the freighter was turned over to U.S. Navy tugs. When they almost lost the *Makedonia* on the rocks, the *Sudbury* took over the tow again and headed for Vancouver, with the freighter's engines turning over at half speed. They encountered 80-mile-per-hour winds and the freighter's propeller came loose again. That same night, in high seas, the towline broke. After a hair-raising night spent connecting a new line, Blagborne decided to proceed to Kodiak, Alaska. Not satisfied with the salvage facilities there, he carried on to Vancouver, encountering heavy seas through Hecate Strait and Queen Charlotte Sound. Forty-one days after leaving Nootka Sound, the *Sudbury* pulled into the Burrard Drydock wharf at Vancouver. The bill for the whole job was $57,341.

In 1956 the *Sudbury* made a similar epic rescue of the Liberty ship *Thunderbird* from mid-Pacific, and two years later brought in the *Andros Legend* when she lost

92. The log barge *Island Hemlock* self-dumping her cargo. She was owned by Island Tug & Barge.

142

her propeller 2,000 miles offshore while coming into Texada Island for a load of ore. That same year Blagborne flew to Australia and brought back an even bigger deep-sea tug purchased by Elworthy, the *Caledonian Salvor,* which had been built to British Admiralty design in 1943 at Napa, California. Elworthy renamed her the *Sudbury II.*

With these two huge tugs, Island Tug's business on the high seas flourished. The company had established a reputation for salvage in a relatively short period of time, between the mid-1950s and the early 1960s. For many reasons, a number of ships wound up in trouble in the north Pacific during that time, and Island Tug, having the best tugs in the area, was

usually called. Also during that time, Island Tug was heavily involved in deep-sea towing, taking old Liberty ships to Japan to be scrapped and bringing back Japanese-built midsections rigged out with false bows to be fitted into existing ships in the United States. When the supply of Liberty ships ran out and business fell off, the *Sudbury* was scrapped. The *Sudbury II* carried on.

The *Sudbury II* also established an enviable salvage reputation. In early 1968 the B.C. Forest Products barge *Forest Prince* went aground on Long Beach on the west coast of Vancouver Island. Heavy swells and a reef held the *Sudbury II* a mile offshore. While the barge cranes were unloading the logs to lighten her, a special

93. Two empty log barges in tow of Straits Towing's *Superior Straits*. She was one of the first diesel electric-powered tugs in B.C. when brought out from the Great Lakes in 1955. The 174-foot tug was originally named the *Abele.*

94. The *Sudbury* pulling the *Andros Legend*, one of the epic salvage tows of the north Pacific, 1958.

6,200-foot towrope was being manufactured in a three-day, round-the-clock operation in Vancouver. One end of the finished towline was dropped onto the barge by helicopter, and at the next high tide the barge was pulled off with little damage.

A less successful voyage was made by the *Sudbury II* in 1974, by which time Island Tug had merged with Vancouver Tug Boat to form Seaspan International Ltd. Harley Blagborne had died of a heart attack while securing a barge in 1969, but he had passed on a lot of knowledge and had trained a number of good people. The new captain was A.J. Fransvagg. The *Sudbury II* left Seattle with a 400-foot log barge in tow, picked up a second barge loaded with lumber in Victoria, headed

for Japan where she exchanged her cargo for oil field pipe, and then left for Point Barrow, Alaska, to join the annual tug and barge flotilla going into Prudhoe Bay. After this, she intended to return to Vancouver; in all, a 12,000-mile voyage. Just out of Japan, the towline to the pipe barge broke, Captain Fransvagg hurt his leg and the tug was forced to drop her barges to rush him back to hospital in Japan. Another captain, Tim Carey, was flown in. The *Sudbury II* picked up the barges which had been watched over by a Japanese tug and continued on her voyage. In the Aleutians, she encountered high seas, and the pipe, valued at more than three million dollars, was swept overboard; one of the barges was capsized and seriously damaged.

95

95. The famed *Sudbury II* (ex-*Caledonian Salvor*) owned by Island Tug & Barge. Her steel-cored towline was two inches in diameter and over half a mile long. Her facilities included a decompression chamber for divers and a machine shop to make spare parts.

96. The barge *Island Maple,* in tow of the *Sudbury,* broke up and sank in high seas off Cape Flattery in October 1963. Both vessels belonged to Island Tug & Barge.

97. The *Sudbury II* rescuing the B.C. Forest Products' log barge *Forest Prince* off the west coast of Vancouver Island, 1968. One end of the specially manufactured towline is being dropped on the tug by helicopter.

There have been, of course, many more marine rescues and salvage operations undertaken by towboats than the ones mentioned here. There are hundreds of cases, many unrecorded, of tugs assisting other boats in trouble. In some instances, tugs incurred expenses or damages that were not covered by their insurance or the insurance of the rescued boats. The rescue function was traditionally and unquestionably the job of any towboat that happened to be able to offer assistance.

This voluntary rescue role was even semiformalized and systematically organized after a series of tragedies at sea. In 1952, the 86-foot steam tug *Petrel* was lost, with all seven crew members, in the tiderips off Cape Mudge. In December 1953, the tug *C.P. Yorke* went down in

Welcome Pass, with a loss of five crew members. A number of other towboats were involved in a variety of accidents around this time, as were scores of fishing boats and pleasure craft. The B.C. Towboat Owners' Association became alarmed. Lives were being lost, insurance rates were climbing and the cost of rescue operations was mounting. Jim Stewart (chairman of the search-and-rescue committee), Bill Atwood, Ray Bicknell, Cecil Cosulich and Cyril Andrews began to organize rescue efforts. In co-operation with the RCAF's search-and-rescue organization, the BCTOA instituted a simple radio-watch program throughout the coastal towboat fleet, at that time numbering about 450 boats. Andrews, a former tug master, was appointed the BCTOA rescue co-ordinator and was granted authority by the towboat companies to divert any of their boats to assist in search-and-rescue operations under the general direction of the RCAF rescue co-ordination centre. An annual $10,000 government grant to the association covered the adminstrative expenses. The system worked well and, at relatively little expense, provided a standby rescue fleet constantly deployed throughout the coastal waters and manned by the most experienced and knowledgeable mariners on the coast. The towboat companies bore the cost of any rescue operation in which they were involved, unless it turned into a salvage or towing job.

In the mid-1950s it was becoming clear that the

98

98. Straits Towing's *Victoria Straits* aground at Merry Island, 1952. The tug is just visible among the rocks at left.

99

99. River tugs, including Bridge Towing's *Chug-away*, on the Fraser River near the Oak Street Bridge, 1952.

100. The *Haida Monarch* (ex-*St. Faith*, ex-*S.D. Brooks*) owned by Kingcome Navigation. Vancouver Tug bought and renamed her the *Le Beau* (second). Kingcome later named its first self-propelled, self-loading, self-dumping log barge the *Haida Monarch*.

aging towboat fleet could not meet the demands of the forest industry and of other users of towboat services. It was also clear that there were not enough war surplus towboats and that many of the converted tugs were simply not adequate for the work. The industry needed smaller, more powerful, better-designed tugs requiring fewer crew members. Vast amounts of capital were needed to equip the industry with proper boats. The federal government was persuaded to provide a forty per cent subsidy to shipyards for the building of new tugs and barges, and their owners were allowed to write off the costs of these vessels against pretax profits over a three-year period.

The result was that a number of tugs and barges were built, some by towboat companies, many by investors having no marine expertise who leased them to towboat companies and claimed the write-off. Unfortunately, some tugs were short, stubby and did not take kindly to the sea. For their size they had very powerful high-speed diesel engines that vibrated the steel hulls unmercifully. And, if the crew was careless with hatch or manhole covers, the tugs had a habit of going to the bottom like stones. Among other things, these tugs were called hot rods and tin cans. Towboaters who had a love and a feel for a good boat hated them with a passion.

Fortunately, well-designed, well-built tugs were coming off the drawing boards of Vancouver naval

Sparkie New
Retired president, Coastal Towing

The *Petrel* went down off Cape Mudge. It was Christmas time—in those days everybody came in for Christmas and went out immediately the holiday was over, so there was always a hell of a crowd of boats going out together.

Well, the *Petrel* was going to Gowland Harbour to pick up a tow of logs there. It was blowing a gale, southeast, and it had been for some time. It was obviously a sustained southeast session of weather that wasn't going to break in the next day or two. But you get going when you can. And there's no problem getting up there anyway.

The *Petrel* was a steamer, so she carried quite a load of water and fuel. And, of course, everyone was getting water and fuel. So Captain Sonum—he was looking after dispatching and was also a member of the firm—told the skipper not to try to get water before he left town, but to go into Lund and get water there to top off his tanks. No sense waiting around with all these boats that were trying to get supplies.

What Sonum had in mind, of course, was that the *Petrel* would be going up the mainland shore. You go up to Lund and when it moderated a bit you'd go across. You couldn't tow logs anyway, so why fight it?

The skipper on the *Petrel* was a damn good skipper, but rather young, and, consequently, he was not too experienced in some things, I suppose. Anyway, he didn't go up to Lund to top off his water tanks, but went straight up the middle of the gulf, and would have arrived off Cape Mudge right in the middle of a great big tide.

The tide comes boiling out of Discovery Passage, drops off, and then comes back. The tide that's coming from the other direction, from Cape Lazo, raises some more hell. But the wind is what really does it, and that night the wind was in the velocity of the seventies and eighties—that's a gale. At that point, of course, the flood goes south against the wind, and the tides meet in that area: the result is a boiling, seething cauldron.

All the evidence indicates that it was a dark night, no moon, and the skipper of the *Petrel* just walked right into this, and she must have gone down like a stone.

The next day nobody knew where she was. She hadn't shown up anywhere and she wasn't at Lund. I started to get pretty anxious and made some inquiries. Somebody said they had noticed an oil slick off Cape Mudge, so I sent the guys out on the *A. G. Garrish*, which was well equipped with sounding equipment. I still have the recordings that the sounder made, showing what had to be the tug lying on the bottom, right at the bottom of a deep V. There was still oil seeping from it. They eventually found the remains of the lifeboat, pulverized on the beach at the cape.

architects like Robert Allan, Gerry Talbot, Derek Cove and Ken Lamont. These men took something of the craftsmanship that had gone into building a classic tug like the *Sea Lion* and combined it with modern materials and equipment, resulting in specialized vessels that were a great improvement on the fairly standardized tug designs of the past.

Kingcome Navigation was one of the companies that undertook a massive new building program which epitomized the trend to new, superior tugs and specialized barges. Kingcome was by this time the towboating arm of MacMillan Bloedel. Thus it was one of the two "captive" towing companies and had specific functions to perform, primarily moving logs and transporting paper from the Powell River and Port Alberni mills. The tendency for such captive towing companies is to perform assigned tasks well, but not to seek innovations or engage in expansion beyond the immediate needs of the parent company. Independent companies, on the other hand, are always on the lookout for new business, improved techniques and ways to expand their capability. The secret of Kingcome's success was the man who ran the company, Bill Dolmage. By 1956, Dolmage was the biggest independent log tower on the coast, and that was the main kind of towing that Dolmage Towing did. In order to expand, he could buy other companies or get into log barging, which was where the future of the towing business lay. He had a

The search-and-rescue service was first organized by the B.C. Towboat Owners' Association. We had a setup going where everybody who had a radio on a boat, including fishermen, was tied in to this system. Cyril Andrews acted as a liaison between the air force and the radio sets on the boats, and people with tugs and so on. He correlated the whole thing and organized it when there was a wreck.

The towboat owners never made any charges for what they did, unless it involved salvage services and there were insurance underwriters involved. We used to render invoices to the association secretary just to keep track of what we had done and what the probable cost of it was. It got into quite a big deal, moneywise.

We had one experience ourselves involving the *Brentwood* which was then in the logging camp service. We got a call to go and assist a seine boat which had capsized somewhere around the mouth of Bull Pass. It seems that she was heading north light and had run over a towline and they'd flipped her over. Three people were trapped inside of her, up in an air pocket and obviously still alive.

There were about three or four tugs helping the *Brentwood*. Our particular job was to keep a strain on the hull to keep her steady and to make sure she didn't roll over or get away, in hopes that we could get her to the beach and do something about getting those men out from inside her.

So we towed all through the night, and at one point—I don't quite know what happened because I wasn't there—she must have swung off a bit one way or the other and carried away our lifting gear. We had five-ton lifting gear there, pretty skookum stuff, but not built for that sort of nonsense.

Repairs cost us about eight thousand dollars, which was covered by insurance, but the loss of the use of our ship while this was going on was near ten thousand dollars, and there was no remuneration for that. It was one of the things you did. There but for the grace of God go I, sort of thing.

This kind of thing happened to many others. When I took over from Doug Coyle as president of the association, he said to me, "Sparkie, you're going to have to do something about air-sea rescue. It's going to break us if you don't." So we persuaded the federal government to give us a grant that year, ten thousand dollars, towards the cost of the thing. From there on they have got into it deeper and deeper and eventually took it over completely.

It was a good deal, because everybody who had a radio was in on the act and there couldn't be an accident that happened anywhere but everybody knew of it. I know several occasions when Cyril Andrews was able to locate boats that I think would otherwise have never shown up again.

101. Island Tug & Barge's *Island Master* at her sea trials in 1967. The 85-foot tug had a twelve-cylinder GM diesel with 1,200 horsepower, and was designed by Robert Allan.

102. The Kingcome Navigation fleet, including (*r. to l.*) the *J.S. Foley* and the *R. Bell-Irving*, on Christmas Day, 1954, with the traditional mast-top trees.

Bill Dolmage

Former president, Dolmage Towing;
retired manager, Kingcome Navigation

When the towboat companies were all talking merger, I was sitting in a great position. I had Crown Zellerbach as one of my best accounts and I had all the outside work at Powell River. I guess we were the major log towers on the coast. I knew I had to get into barging, so I went to a large timber company that was going in on the west coast. I talked to them and they were willing to give me a fantastic contract if I built barges to service them. I'd have no trouble getting the money for something like that, a ten-year charter.

But I thought to myself, my outfit's all paid for and I don't owe a bean to anybody. I'm fifty years of age, why do I want to go out and borrow a million or two million dollars? Just a big headache.

One company was keen to buy me. As a matter of fact, I was all set to buy Victoria Tugboats. It wasn't such a lot then, just two or three boats and six or eight scows. But this company was also very keen on getting Victoria Tug, and I had an option to buy it.

Vancouver Tug were keen to get me, too, because they had all the Crown Zellerbach scow towing—paper from Ocean Falls and so forth—as their best account. I was getting in thicker and thicker with Crown all the time and it was bothering Vancouver Tug. I guess they figured I was a lot better out of the way so they made me a good offer and I took it. I don't regret it.

As it turned out, it was a wise move, because there was a real slump right after that. Log towing just went to pieces. Everybody had tough going for a while. That must have been in 1956 or 1957.

Nobody had the cash to put up the bill for new equipment, but there was good management. Some people wanted to get out and get their money out. We were all getting to the stage where we wanted to get out and let some younger people take over.

third choice, to sell out, which he did. He then took on the job of running Kingcome Navigation.

If the executives at MacMillan Bloedel had wanted a conventional "captive" towing operation, they made the wrong choice when they hired Bill Dolmage. By the time he left Kingcome fifteen years later, the company and the marine transportation industry on the B.C. coast had been radically transformed. The first new boats were clearly recognizable as tugs: the *Harmac Pine* and the *Harmac Spruce* were both 65-foot, 750-horsepower steel tugs built by John Manly Shipyard in 1964. The same year, two 365-foot covered barges for carrying newsprint were built. They were followed two

103. The *Harmac Pine* owned by Kingcome Navigation, 1964. The 65-foot, 750-horsepower tug was built by John Manly.

years later by a 140-foot oceangoing tug, the *Haida Brave*, designed to tow newsprint barges from Port Alberni to Los Angeles. Dolmage had wanted a 165-foot tug but settled for less. She had 3,500 horsepower in her twin Stork-Werkspoor diesels and was built in Nova Scotia by Halifax Shipyards. She was sailed around to British Columbia via the Panama Canal.

At this juncture, Kingcome advanced well beyond the traditional towboat-and-barge technique with the *Haida Transporter*, a self-propelled railcar barge designed by Gerry Talbot. She was built to haul cars of newsprint from Powell River to Vancouver and was so

104

103

105

104. Underwater photograph of the name board of the *Emerald Straits*, before she was raised, taken from the mini-submarine *Pisces*.

105. Raising the diesel tug *Emerald Straits* (Straits Towing) in Howe Sound, 1969. The 51-foot steel boat was launched in 1950.

successful that she also performed the same function for the Harmac mill at Nanaimo and still had time left over to make a weekly trip or two for the CPR between Vancouver Island and the mainland. The most revolutionary vessel that Kingcome built was the enormous self-loading, self-propelled, self-dumping log barge *Haida Monarch*, which went into the water in 1974. Designed by Gerry Talbot, she was 430 feet long and run by a twelve-man crew. With an awesome 7,200 horsepower, she could travel at 12 knots while carrying a 15,000-ton cargo. She could load in eighteen hours with her two derricks and unload by flooding her tanks in only half an hour. And she cost $10 million. Four years later, a similar but slightly smaller barge was launched, taking the name of the tug *Haida Brave*, which had been sold to RivTow Straits Ltd. and renamed the *RivTow Commodore*.

The transformation of Kingcome's fleet was an indication of what faced towing companies if they wanted to stay in business. They had to have new boats and be prepared to find the capital to get them. They needed expensive, specialized barges to haul logs, chips and other wood products, chemicals and fuel. And they had to be able to operate in the big league of the multinational corporate business structure which was evolving around them.

106. Kingcome Navigation's *Haida Carrier*, with its two huge derricks circa 1964. Also at the dock are (*l. to r.*): *Ednorina* and *Caribou*, *Sea Spray* and *Sea Dawn* (Noble Towing), *Haulaway*, *Sea Pilot* and *Sea Coaster* (Pacific Towing Services), *M.R. Cliff*.

8 / Mergers, Sellouts and Takeovers

Between 1950 and 1970, a complicated series of sellouts, mergers and takeovers took place in the towboat industry, resulting in a complete reorganization. The first decade of this process ended with the emergence of five companies which had swallowed most of those in existence at the end of World War II. The second decade ended with two giant towing corporations dominating the industry.

In 1950, Stan McKeen of Straits Towing took over Pacific Salvage and reorganized the companies so that Straits devoted itself to towing while Pacific concentrated on salvage operations. McKeen also took over Pacific Coyle Navigation in 1956. Meanwhile, his ex-partner Harold Elworthy was expanding Island Tug & Barge by taking over Young and Gore in 1952 and Victoria Tugboats in 1959.

On the Fraser River, River Towing (owned by Cecil Cosulich) and Pioneer Towing (owned by Bill Dolmage, Ron Wilson and Bill Atwood) each took over half of Paul Raake Boat Services and changed the name to Raake Marine Services. In 1955, Pioneer Towing bought Towers Towing and its five tugs. When Bill Dolmage went to Kingcome Navigation in 1956, River Towing bought Dolmage's interest in Pioneer Towing. Then Cecil Cosulich joined with Bill Atwood and Ron Wilson to buy up the somewhat antiquated M.R. Cliff Tugboat Company. Other action on the Fraser included the purchase by Evans, Coleman and Evans (later Ocean Construction) of Gilley Bros., an old river towing company which had absorbed Marpole Towing.

The Vancouver Tug Boat Company was also expanding, under the direction of Harold Jones. His

107. The *Red Fir No. 5* and the *Red Fir No. 8* on the Fraser River.

108

109

107

108. The river tug *Haulaway*, owned successively by Towers Towing, Pioneer Towing and RivTow Marine.

109. The 45-foot *River Belle* was a U.S. war surplus tug brought to B.C. by Capilano Towing, an affiliate of Pioneer Towing.

110. Vancouver Tug Boat's *Le Prince* (second) with a tandem tow of flat scows loaded with houses, leaving the Fraser River en route to Stewart, 1965. Vancouver Tug bought the first *Le Prince* (as the *Sea Prince*) from Dolmage Towing.

success was partly due to the strong, competent management structure that he had created. Arthur Lindsay was executive vice-president, and under him was a former tug captain, Jim Stewart, vice-president of operations, as well as his own son, Rod Lindsay, general manager. In 1956, Vancouver Tug bought Dolmage Towing, Bill Dolmage's coastal log-towing company, when he went to Kingcome. For a year, Dolmage Towing was operated as a separate entity called Vancouver Log Towing under the management of Bill Atwood and Cornelius Burke, then was absorbed into Vancouver Tug.

By the end of the 1950s, there were five strong companies—Straits Towing, Island Tug & Barge, River Towing, Vancouver Tug, and Gulf of Georgia Towing—plus a host of smaller companies which were not in the running for the takeover or merger stakes.

The 1960s began with the sale of Island Tug to McAllister Towing of Montreal, which was in turn owned by Sogemines, a Canadian company (started with Belgian money) with headquarters also in Montreal. The Elworthy family was retained under a ten-year management agreement. The following year, Island Tug bought out the Griffiths Steamship Company. The next few years were relatively quiet and few of the major companies changed hands. They needed their energy to consolidate their holdings and to fight for survival in the ruthless competition that

111

111. Three of Vancouver Tug's boats pulling a span of the CNR railway bridge into place across Second Narrows, circa 1968.

developed after anticombines legislation ended their gentlemen's agreement to charge common rates except on contract bidding.

Vancouver Tug continued to expand after Harold Jones died late in 1956. Arthur Lindsay took over as president until 1959 when he became chairman; Jim Stewart then became the chief executive officer on through the hectic years that followed. These included the acquisition of Vancouver Barge Transportation in 1962, Pacific Tanker Company in 1964, and Western Tug & Barge from Harry Hansen and Bob Wilson in 1965. That year, Vancouver Tug made a very important and timely decision. It bought the Domtar property at the foot of Pemberton Avenue in North Vancouver and drew up plans for operating headquarters, fleet moorage and a modern shipyard equipped for lifting tugs and barges out of the water and conveying them by a rail transfer system to appropriate points on land where maintenance and repair could most effectively be carried out. This was known as the syncrolift system, the first application in Canada, and it gave the company effective control over its fast-growing fleet of 26 tugs with up to 3,600 horsepower and 155 barges of up to 9,000-ton carrying capacity.

The management team of Vancouver Tug under Jim Stewart in 1967 was composed of vice-presidents Rod Lindsay, Norm McCarvill and John Pearson, and the manager of the new Vancouver Shipyards, Allen

112

112. Vancouver Tug's *La Pointe* (ex-*Kingsway*) towing the Alaska cruise boat *Princess Louise* out of Vancouver harbour, 1966. The 6,000-ton, 317-foot cruise ship was towed to Long Beach, California, where she was converted into a floating restaurant.

James S. Byrn
President, Genstar Marine

I was fortunate to work on the tugs in the late thirties while on summer holidays. At thirteen I was a mess boy, and a nuisance, for ten cents a day. At fifteen I became a deck hand at one dollar per day (thirty dollars per month for thirty days worked).

Then, in 1941 I joined the RCAF, became a pilot until VE Day, then back to UBC, and in 1949 returned to Gulf of Georgia as office boy.

Gulf of Georgia Towing Company—Gulf—had been purchased by my father Stav Byrn and my uncle Ray Bicknell in 1943. (Dad and Uncle Ray had started to work with Gulf in 1930 and 1929 respectively.) The company had about fifty wooden barges and five tugs with 50 to 150 horsepower at that time. Gulf started to change from the towing of logs in flat rafts and bundle booms to the towing of barges and it built up a fleet of about three hundred wooden barges, which were leased directly to the forest industry and other towing companies.

Gulf grew in the fifties and sixties to be the third largest marine towing company—Seaspan was first, RivTow second—with a fleet of twelve steel tugs ranging from harbour tugs of 500 horsepower to oceangoing tugs of 3,200 horsepower, and a fleet of seventy steel barges with 2,000 to 8,000 tons carrying capacity. These barges carried chemicals like caustic or chlorine, light and heavy oil, chips, pulp and paper, limestone, gravel and general cargoes.

I purchased Gulf from my father and my Uncle Ray in 1963.

When you're an aggressive independent owner, after a while you reach a ceiling in financing because the industry does not have a large return. You either have to stop growing and consolidate, or specialize in one particular portion of the industry, or sell out. So, slowly, people like the Yorkes and McKeens, when they had a good offer, sold out. They had worked hard all their lives, often through two or three generations, and now felt they should take the cash and find other areas in which to invest.

I sold out for the same reasons. I had pretty well reached the limit that I could expand. I had offers to sell many times during the late sixties and early seventies but I wasn't ready. Genstar came in 1977, and I felt they offered me a fair deal and they would look after all my people. This was important, as we had second- and third-generation employees, and my life had been the growing up with them. We'd gone from a company of less than a hundred people in the sixties to four hundred and fifty people in the mid-seventies. I just saw it as an opportunity for our people to be looked after and, as it happened, I was able to stay in the industry.

Now, the major companies are so large it is very hard for senior executives to keep the close relationships with their crews that they had in the past. This closeness was one of the strengths of the towing companies, as they competitively grew through the last thirty years.

However, today, with large diversified marine companies, it is harder for new employees to develop the same allegiances to an individual owner as in the past. To fill this void, many employees have turned to their fraternal organizations, the guild or union that does the bargaining for them. So another change has started.

People talk of "how great it was in the past"— and it was. First of all, the industry was not as highball, because costs and wages were much lower. Several tugs and barges might take two or three days to do what is done today with one tug and one barge in maybe a little over a day. The industry, because of conditions and much higher costs, has been forced to become very efficient. The old days of fishlines over the side when towing, accordion playing on the back deck, with regular tie-ups for weather and tide, are just things to talk about.

Today's towboat operations, with constantly changing crews, and more time off and away from the job than on, make it harder for strong fellowships to develop. With the constant rotation of people for time off, seniority changes, holidays, sickness and social functions, the same crew units are very seldom able to be kept together.

The happy leisure living together of the past created a strong fellowship among the whole crew. They worked as a unit and worked well, enjoying the job and each other.

Fowlis (later president of Seaspan), who was responsible for supervising the construction of the yard. In 1969, Vancouver Tug bought an adjacent piece of property, allowing the shipyard to expand into building tugs and barges. This considerably strengthened the company's control over both operating and capital costs, and made it very attractive to both Canadian and American acquisition-minded companies.

Gulf of Georgia Towing, under Ray Bicknell and Stavert Byrn, kept clear of the company buying spree and concentrated on expanding its barge fleet. Soon it owned about three hundred barges and six or seven tugs. In 1963, the company was taken over by Stavert's son, Jim, who concentrated very successfully on long-term contract bidding.

In 1964 the various companies that the Cosulichs had acquired were consolidated under the name of RivTow Marine. The name was a subtle way of announcing that the company was now operating outside the confines of the Fraser River. The combined assets of River Towing, M.R. Cliff Tugboat, Canyon Towing, Towers Towing, Pioneer Towing and Raake Marine Services gave RivTow eight tugs on the Skeena River and twenty-five tugs on the Fraser River, as well as the beginnings of a coastal fleet of tugs and barges. This consolidated operation established RivTow as a serious contender in the fight for control of the towing industry.

One new company, Pacific Towing Services, was formed in 1964 by Ron Wilson, who had one tug in Chieftain Towing, and Lance Higgs, who had a tug in Knight Towing. The company was set up to act as an operating vehicle for these two towing companies. Wilson and Higgs were joined at the start by Bill Atwood, who had been involved in a number of towing companies, including Dolmage Towing, Pioneer Towing and Vancouver Tug Boat. In 1965, Pacific Towing bought Bendickson Towing, and continued to expand over the years. Lance Higgs left the company in 1971, taking with him the tug *Pacific Challenge*, the last steam tug to operate in B.C. waters. She had been built in 1952 in Norway as a whaler, with a double compound steam engine. Higgs took her down to Puerto Rico, where she engaged in towing for some years until her steam engines gave out; she was towed back to Vancouver and repowered with a 3,600-

horsepower GM diesel engine. She stayed to work in B.C. and for several years towed barges for Seaspan International, then for the White Pass and Yukon Railway. Recently, she towed paper barges down to Los Angeles for Kingcome Navigation.

In 1965, Peter Shields, a civil engineer involved in marine construction, started a towing company called Shields Navigation with the *Coal Island*, a landing barge. Over the next few years his company developed a diversified business focussed on a barging operation which combined fuel delivery and equipment moving to coastal logging camps. The company also moved into barging gravel, laying submarine telephone and hydroelectric cables, and log barging.

On a slightly different note, two more forest companies established towing subsidiaries by buying existing companies in 1967. B.C. Forest Products bought Swiftsure Towing from Jack Bruno, and Weldwood took over Escott Towing from Thor Larsen and Fred Lemoine.

In addition to their resolute attempts to raise the capital required to build much-needed modern equipment, the five major companies were jockeying for power and control in the industry. It rapidly became clear that there was not enough room to permit all the companies to expand. The closing years of the 1960s featured a number of discreet meetings, tentative offers and counteroffers among the main participants. Also, major towing companies and marine-oriented conglomerates in eastern Canada and in the United States were becoming aware that the major towing companies in British Columbia, with its rapidly expanding economy, could not provide the capital to build the new equipment needed. In other words, the climate was right for takeover bids from corporations knowledgeable about marine operations.

The first major move took place in 1969, when the Dillingham Corporation of Honolulu, owners of Hawaiian Tug and Barge, bought Foss Launch and Tug of Seattle and its subsidiary, Pacific Tow Boat; later that year, Dillingham announced that it had acquired all the shares of Vancouver Tug Boat Company.

Underlying all these high-level manoeuvres was the realization that relations between owners and crews had to be resolved before the industry could become truly stable. The contracts of the the three towboat unions were all coming up for renewal in 1970, and the crews who manned the boats were far from happy. After several months of fruitless negotiations between the B.C. Towboat Owners' Association and the unions —the Canadian Merchant Service Guild, representing 1,300 masters, mates and engineers; the Seafarers International Union and the Canadian Brotherhood of Railway, Transport and General Workers, representing 700 deck hands, oilers and cooks—the guild went on strike in May 1970. It quickly became a battle between the guild and the owners; the other two unions pulled back to await the outcome.

The issues at stake were complex and bound up with the past twenty years of the industry's history:

wages were important, as were safety and working conditions. The guild was also concerned about the many changes of ownership, which at that point showed no sign of ending. It asked for a role in these transactions, insisting that the contract between the guild and the owners was on a boat-by-boat basis and that if a boat were sold, the contract remained in force.

Manning was also a major issue, as it had been for the past twenty years while the companies sought to reduce the number of men in a crew. The manning question was part of the overriding issue of the strike: safety. The guild argued that three- or four-man boats were expected to do the same kind of work that six- or seven-man boats had performed a few years earlier.

113

113. Towboat workers picketing at Port Mellon during the 1970 strike.

Much of the safety argument centred on some of the tugs that had been built during the previous fifteen years. The guild argued that these small, powerful, steel-hulled boats were pulling barges of ever-increasing size.

The guild's concern certainly had some justification. In the previous five years, twenty-nine men had lost their lives on two- and three-man boats, and fifty boats had been sunk. The guild pointed out that twenty-four of these twenty-nine men had died in steel-hulled boats, though only twenty-one of the fifty boats sunk had been built of steel. In the midst of negotiations, a confidential federal government report was circulated; it contended that eighty per cent of the tugs and half of the men on them were constantly exposed to unsatisfactory conditions. The survey of fifty boats, not all owned by BCTOA members, condemned excessive working hours, unsafe practices, inadequate crew quarters, poor feeding and sanitary arrangements, and dangers arising from the basically unsafe design of some tugs.

The owners' position on the safety issue was that a large proportion of the accidents had been caused by carelessness: poor navigation practices, life jackets not being worn, and watertight doors and hatches left open. The government report also substantiated the arguments put forward by tug owners.

114

114. The Stone Bros. dock at Port Alberni. The whole fleet is tied up at dock because of the 1970 strike.

Both sides in the dispute started out with professional negotiators, but this situation rapidly altered. The guild's representative was dismissed and sent back to Ottawa. His place was taken by Arnie Davis, captain of Kingcome Navigation's *Haida Chieftain*. Although the BCTOA retained its negotiator, its side of the battle was represented, at least in public, by Rod Lindsay, president of the association and vice-president of Vancouver Tug. It had turned into quite a confrontation: one side was represented by the captain of one of the most powerful tugs on the coast, and the other side by one of the most able and respected managers in the business.

Within a week of the strike's commencement, a third of the coastal forest industry was shut down. The B.C. Federation of Labour lined up solidly behind the guild and, by the time another two weeks had passed, most forest operations had come to a halt. The construction industry, which was dependent on tug transportation for building materials, was also affected, as were coastal airline companies, equipment companies and suppliers. In less than one month, about 20,000 people were out of work. If nothing else was made clear in this strike, it became obvious to everyone in British Columbia that the towboat industry is the lifeline of the provincial economy. That such a small industry in terms of capital investment and the number of employees could play such a vital role in the provincial economy came as a shock to many people—except, of course, to those in the towboat industry. As the reality became dramatically evident and the rest of the labour movement showed no sign of slackening its support, some of the affected forest companies launched a series of injunctions and contempt proceedings against the guild. Within a few days, the courts ordered the seizure of the office and assets of the guild and Arnie Davis was jailed for contempt of court. A few days later a settlement was reached and the strike ended. In the final agreement, many of the guild's demands were met to some degree, but not the one calling for participation in the sale of companies and boats. Less than a month later, the mergers creating Seaspan International and RivTow Straits were announced.

RivTow Marine announced that it was merging with Straits Towing and that the new venture would be called RivTow Straits. Fred Brown of Straits Towing

became chairman of the company and Cecil Cosulich of RivTow was president. Norman Cosulich and George McKeen, whose grandfather had been a towboater in the last century, became vice-presidents. Lucille Johnstone, who had been a tug dispatcher for Silver Skagit Logging before joining River Towing in the early 1940s as a secretary for the Cosulichs, was appointed vice-president of administration. She was responsible for financing acquisitions as RivTow began to expand and diversify, and eventually she became a senior vice-president and secretary of the board. The newly created company, with $20 million in assets, 225 pieces of floating equipment and 750 employees, dwarfed every other towing operation on the coast, except Seaspan.

115. The *Chikugo Maru* leaving Roberts Bank assisted by Seaspan tugs (*l. to r.*): *Island Master, Valiant, La Garde, La Salle, Island King.*

116

The creation of Seaspan International was announced two weeks later. It came about through a deal worked out between two international corporations, Dillingham and Genstar (formerly Sogemines), to merge their two properties, Vancouver Tug and Island Tug & Barge respectively. The combined operation was called Vancouver Island Tug and Barge until, by using a logical-name process on a computer, Jacques Heyrman, an executive assistant, came up with the more imaginative name of Seaspan International. The new company owned more than 250 barges and 65 tugs and employed about 1,100 people. Arthur Elworthy was chairman of the board and Jim Stewart was president.

115

116. The Straits Towing fleet tied up for Christmas, including (*centre to r.*): the *Salvage Queen*, the *Charlotte Straits*, the *Commodore Straits*.

117. The 41-foot *Regent*, running light up the Fraser River, was built in 1970 by Vito Steel Boat and Barge Construction to a Robert Allan design for Regent Towing. The tug later was acquired by RivTow.

The twin mergers that created Seaspan International and RivTow Straits in 1970 indicated the extent to which an industry highly diversified in its ownership had now become almost oligopolistic in nature. With a few notable exceptions, the family-owned and -operated companies had disappeared. These two mergers established the pattern or structure of the industry that has prevailed until the present time. They by no means marked the end of the acquisition process; more mergers and takeovers followed during the next seven years. But the primary emphasis within the industry was on consolidating the ownership structure which had been so drastically altered during the previous decade.

The industry also had to deal with the effects of the 1970 towboat strike. This event had seriously disrupted the coastal economy, demonstrating dramatically that an industry employing only 2,000 was critical in the maintenance of other industries employing tens of thousands of people. There was widespread concern outside the industry regarding the future stability of the coast's main transportation facility. The forest companies were particularly concerned and, as was demonstrated by the entry of B.C. Forest Products and Weldwood into the towing business, were willing to take care of their own marine transportation needs if they thought that the independent towing companies were unable to do so.

It was also clear that, if the spirit of the settlement reached with the guild and the unions was to be honoured, a large amount of energy and dollars had to be invested to develop better boats and equipment, to create better working conditions and to re-establish harmony within the industry. Related to this was the need to improve the industry's safety record, both for the sake of its employees and to satisfy the rapidly expanding demands of government regulatory agencies.

During the 1970s, the two major towing companies had several disquieting internal difficulties to resolve. Seaspan was owned jointly by two international corporations and consisted of an uneasy melding of two formerly powerful companies, Island Tug and Vancouver Tug (not to mention the smaller companies that had previously been absorbed into both). They did not keep these names, but at the working level there still existed strong loyalties to old companies, which had

been quite different in the type of work they had performed and the style in which they had done it. And the management level consisted of the Elworthy brothers from Island Tug and executives of Vancouver Tug, chiefly Jim Stewart and Rod Lindsay. Island Tug, traditionally, had been a tight, family-run operation engaged primarily in barging, deep-sea towing and salvage, based in Victoria. Vancouver Tug, on the other hand, had been a Vancouver company run by a group of experienced managers who, for the most part, had worked their way up through the ranks. Although it too had been a barging company, it had a short log-towing tradition from its acquisition of Dolmage Towing in the 1950s.

A similar situation existed at RivTow Straits. The RivTow part of the operation was controlled by the Cosulichs, who were used to towing in the muddy currents of the Fraser River. Straits Towing, controlled by the McKeen and Brown families, was oriented to coastal towing.

Despite such internal difficulties, the two majors were competing for dominance of the industry. One strong company, Gulf of Georgia Towing, was still outside their control. Given the climate created by the previous mergers, there was a widespread feeling that whoever succeeded in taking over Gulf of Georgia would dominate the industry.

RivTow continued to expand by acquisition. In 1971 it picked up Armour Salvage, Great West Towing & Salvage and the major interest in Bute Towing. The following year, RivTow began to diversify and bought three shipbuilding firms: John Manly, B.C. Marine and West Coast Salvage.

Seaspan was also keen to expand, but was finding decision-making much more difficult because its two shareholders, each owning fifty per cent, had different financial and philosophical attitudes towards business: Genstar's very eastern Canadian and European, and Dillingham's very American. In the fall of 1971 an outsider to the industry, Ross Turner, past president of a large diversified company, was made president of Seaspan to deal with problems of administration and expansion, and to free Jim Stewart to run the towing business. In 1972, Seaspan bought F.M. Yorke & Son, a company that had been founded in 1920 and had pioneered the barging of railcars to Vancouver Island.

The assets of F.M. Yorke & Son included eight barges, two self-propelled barges—the *Doris Yorke* and the *Greg Yorke*—and a tug, the 94-foot *Lorne Yorke*. Early in 1973, Seaspan, Federal Commerce and Navigation of Montreal and Crowley Maritime of San Francisco established the Arctic Transportation Company to operate in the western Arctic. A few months later Dillingham sold its share of Seaspan to Genstar; Ross Turner was made president of Genstar Western Ltd. (which oversaw Seaspan) and eventually president of the giant Genstar corporation. Rod Lindsay became president of Seaspan and Jim Stewart stayed on as chairman and chief executive officer. Seaspan undertook a second joint international venture with Crowley and Union Remarque de Sauvetage, a Belgian company, in the North Sea, followed by a third with Crowley and Federal Commerce and Navigation in Saudia Arabia and the Mediterranean.

The Arctic Transportation Company venture provided towboaters in British Columbia with a new field of operations. The style of this undertaking, however, was not at all reminiscent of the rough-and-ready pioneer days of towboating, but was a complex, highly organized and well-equipped expedition through the Arctic sea ice. The first convoy of towboats went into the Arctic in 1968, when Arctic Marine Freighters, a consortium of U.S. towing companies, sent a fleet with the first commercial cargo to go around Point Barrow, bound for the Prudhoe Bay oil fields in Alaska. This operation was the first of a series of annual supply missions to the area. In 1970, eighteen tugs and sixty-two barges took in 187,000 tons of supplies to the North Slope of Alaska. The tricky part of this venture was to assemble the tug and barge fleet near Point Barrow by late July, ready to dash through the narrow channels that the offshore winds usually opened through the sea ice during August. Then navigation might be possible for a month or two, but there was always the chance that the ice would not open at all.

The bulk of Canadian supplies to the Arctic go inland via the Mackenzie River. The Americans still run regular convoys into the Arctic around Point Barrow, but there have been only occasional B.C. expeditions into the area. In 1973 the Arctic Transportation Company undertook to convoy a fleet of B.C. tugs and barges from Vancouver to Tuktoyaktuk at the mouth of the Mackenzie River. The *Seaspan Navigator*, the *Seaspan Commander* and the *Seaspan Mariner* accompanied four shallow-draft river tugs and fourteen barges being delivered to the area. It was a 3,700-mile tow from Vancouver, but the worst of it was a five-mile stretch through the ice floes off Point Barrow in a run co-ordinated with the annual U.S. convoy to Alaska. Reconnaissance aircraft were used to find channels through the ice, bringing that particular operation to a successful conclusion.

In the midst of the mad scramble on the part of RivTow and Seaspan to take over every company in sight, a couple of events indicated that there was still a lot of life in other quarters of the towing industry. In 1974, Pacific Towing Services bought the Stone Bros. operation in Port Alberni, consisting of eight tugs and a subsidiary shipyard. Pacific Towing has become one of the major independents in the industry, with 120 employees, twelve tugs (five based in Vancouver, seven in Port Alberni), a shipyard and log-sorting areas. The company engages in general towing work but specializes in towing log booms. Another important function is ship docking in Port Alberni, where its tugs berth up to 300 vessels a year. Also in the mid-1970s, Pacific Logging, the forest products wing of the CPR, bought Chemainus Towing to look after its own towing needs, chiefly log transport.

In 1975 RivTow Straits took over Point Grey Towing, and added ninety-five per cent of the Cooper family's Westminster Tug Boats the following year. By this time, RivTow was a prime mover of forest products on the B.C. coast. Its tugs were also towing barges in faraway places such as Japan, Singapore, the Atlantic coast, the North Sea and the Arctic. It was involved in a joint venture called Arctic Navigation and Transportation, towing on the Mackenzie River and along the Arctic coast. It also continued to diversify into a number of other business areas.

The economics of the towboat industry were changing. Equipment costs had escalated greatly, in part because bigger and more specialized tugs and barges were required, and because of inflation. A chip barge in the late 1960s had cost between $50,000 and $100,000; ten years later the larger barges required for the business cost close to $400,000. During the 1970s, tug prices doubled. These soaring costs made it hard for an

118. The *Gibraltar Straits* (*centre foreground*) tending an oil rig in the North Sea. She was owned
by Straits Towing, then by RivTow Straits.

independent company to secure financing once it had reached a certain debt level. The return on investment in the towing industry was not high enough to support the kind of growth and internal expansion required during this period. Most of the independent companies were faced with the choice of limiting their growth and consolidating their operations, or of selling out.

Gulf of Georgia Towing was in such a position. It had remained a strong, independent company, and in 1977 had 450 employees, up from 100 in 1967. It was primarily a barging company, with a fleet of 250 barges hauling lumber, logs, chemicals, petroleum products, building materials, railcars and limestone. Its largest tug, *Gulf Joan*—a 3,000-horsepower, 149-foot deep-sea

tug—was used to service the first offshore drilling rig in Canada, the largest mobile offshore drilling unit in the world. The same tug was used to tow ships throughout the Pacific. In spite of its healthy position, the days of the Gulf of Georgia company were numbered. Without additional capital it could not grow much more, and to stop growing would, in the long run, mean losing business to Seaspan and RivTow Straits, which could raise the capital needed to build the multimillion-dollar log barges and sophisticated tugs now required. So, in 1977, after turning down a number of offers, Jim Byrn sold Gulf of Georgia to Seaspan and was appointed president of Genstar Marine, Seaspan's owner.

This transaction pretty well concluded the merger

119. The *Naskeena 4*, a 35-foot, 480-horsepower tug owned by RivTow.

James S. Byrn
President, Genstar Marine

All west coast towing companies have had many changes to their operations between 1940 and the present date. Slowly, in the late forties, horsepower was increased in many of the older and larger tugs to 200 to 400 horsepower. Wooden barges also changed from the standard 30 by 80 feet to 36 by 110 feet, an increase in carrying capacity from 80 to 350 tons.

In the mid-fifties the industry started to change over to steel construction for tugs and barges. Barges were built for specific needs: petroleum carriers for the major oil companies; chemical, chip, hog fuel and covered-house barges in the early 1960s; and self-loading and self-propelled log ships in the mid-1970s.

Changes in costs started to occur, causing operators to move to bigger equipment. One result was a major breakthrough for crews of seven days per month off, graduating to ten days per month off.

The cost of barges has escalated greatly over the last twenty years. This was caused by the increased size of equipment and inflation. For example: Gulf built smaller chip barges, 43 by 150 feet, for $50,000 to $100,000 in the mid-sixties. Today a chip barge is 50 by 210 feet and costs about $950,000. Seaspan's new self-loading and unloading log barge, the *Seaspan Rigger*, is capable of lifting fifty-ton bundles. It cost in excess of ten million dollars.

Tug costs have also escalated. In 1965, an 800-horsepower coastal tug cost about $500,000. In 1974, a 1,500-horsepower coastal tug was $950,000. Today a 2,200-horsepower coastal tug, depending on sophistication, is three to five million dollars.

and takeover process that had been going on in the industry for more than twenty years. An inquiry by the Combines Investigation branch of the federal government concluded that the Seaspan acquisition of Gulf of Georgia did not restrict competition within the industry. And with Gulf of Georgia out of the running, the towing industry achieved a certain stability. Since then, neither RivTow nor Seaspan has bought any more towing companies, though both have continued to expand internally. The Cosulichs bought out the McKeen and Brown interests in RivTow Straits, turning the firm into a family-operated business. While maintaining its position as the province's second largest towboating company, RivTow has continued a deliberate diversifica-

120. Gulf of Georgia Towing's *Gulf Joan* towing a Shell Oil drilling rig, *Sedco 135*, near Victoria harbour, 1967.

tion policy. In addition to shipbuilding, it has moved into industrial equipment (Western Tractor, RivQuip, Purves Ritchie, Coneco), gravel and concrete (Pacific Rim Aggregate) and real estate.

The stability that developed after the sale of Gulf of Georgia Towing meant that a number of smaller companies were able to consolidate their financial positions and expand within clearly defined areas. C.H. Cates & Sons, which now does all the ship berthing in Burrard Inlet, is a prime example. It is still a family-owned operation, run by Terry Waghorn, a son-in-law of John Cates, whose father Charles H. was steaming around the harbour in a tug long before the turn of the century. It is unlikely that anyone would consider trying to compete with the Cates operation. Not only do their crews know every nook, cranny and back eddy of the harbour, but they also have a specialized fleet of fourteen ship-berthing tugs that would be difficult and costly to match. On the other hand, it is doubtful that the Cates people would attempt to use these specialized tugs, particularly the newer ones, on any other job. Their newest boats, the *Charles H. Cates V, VI, VII* and *VIII*, are 60-foot, 1,800-horsepower twin screw harbour tugs. Their housework is positioned and sloped so that they can get in under the flared hulls of freighters and liners while pushing them into or away from the wharves. The wheelhouses are designed for maximum visibility and, instead of towing winches, they have

120

121

121. The *Gulf Margaret* (Gulf of Georgia Towing) towing flat barge *GG 290* loaded with the remains of a crashed airliner, 1968.

electrically operated quick-release hooks to which lines from the ships are attached for towing. These are two-man boats with no sleeping accommodations.

The hazards of ship berthing are unique and relate to the problems of a 60-foot tug of 66 gross tons packing 1,800 horsepower trying to manoeuvre a superfreighter like the *Amoco Cairo*, which is 960 feet long and can hold 4.8 million bushels of wheat and 20,000 tons of rapeseed. A whole variety of things can go wrong when trying to berth such a huge ship, or even one that is much smaller. The tide can catch the ship and drive it against the wharf, crushing the tug. One Cates tug was swamped by the wash from a ship's propeller when her captain unexpectedly went ahead on

his engines. Other tugs have been dragged backward and rolled over while towing a ship that surges slightly one way or another under its own power. The captain of a harbour tug is a nervous man when lines from a ship are attached to his tug. Hence the quick-release hook, which can be instantly activated by hitting a button in the wheelhouse.

On the other hand, Pacific Towing Services, with twelve tugs, successfully competes with the two big companies and the forest company affiliates for general towing work. The same is true of a number of other smaller independent firms. Shields Navigation, with six tugs and a self-propelled barge, the *Georgia Transporter*, moves equipment and fuel all over the

122. The *Kaymar* owned by Pacific Towing Services
at a booming ground.

coast. North Arm Transportation barges twenty million gallons of fuel a year to logging and mining operations on the west coast of Vancouver Island, the north coast and the Queen Charlotte Islands. Harken Towing with seven boats, Hodder Tugboat with five and Valley Towing with eight all operate on the Fraser River.

In addition to these small towing operations there are as many as two hundred owner-operated tugs. Some owner-operators have contracts with the larger companies or with the forest companies to perform certain limited jobs. Others operate on a free-lance basis: they pick up odd towing jobs, engage in a bit of beach-combing for logs lost out of booms, or do some hand-logging on the side. Most of the boats in this sector of the industry have been bought from the bigger companies.

The big companies have an ambivalent attitude towards these owner-operated independents. Working outside the reach of the unions and, often, the regulatory agencies of the government, they are frequently able to undercut the rates charged by the established firms. Their independence is an attractive feature for the forest companies, who see in them a form of insurance in the event of a towboat strike. At the same time, there is a certain tolerance and respect for them, owing no doubt to the knowledge that just about every towboat company on the coast had its origins in a similar hard-working venture.

123

124

123. The *Stormforce* owned by Shields Navigation, 1976. She is a 67-foot tug with 1,450 horse-power.

124. Inside the wheelhouse of the *Stormforce*.

Doug Stone

Former president, Stone Bros.

One of the first jobs my great-grandfather had was turning spars for the sailing ships. He had a huge lathe with a couple of horses to run it—they went round and round and turned the lathe through a system of gearing. The spars were held between centres, and there was a bowed sort of guide that allowed a man to walk along with his chisel. It would turn out spars that were thicker in the middle and tapered gradually to the ends.

My great-grandfather was not exactly in the towing business, but he had sailing barges and used to carry on a trade between Holland and England. I heard tell that he had a primitive sort of steam tug, with side wheels, but he didn't think there was much future for it. He operated out of a little town, Erith, just below London.

My grandfather had the very first oil-engine tug on the Thames River. It was a little tug called the *Union*. It had a two-cylinder, thirty-horsepower Ackroyd engine. The cylinder lay flat, something like a Volkswagen engine. The smokestack, with a muffler on it, would fold down flat on the deck. The wheelhouse was a tarpaulin on four stanchions. When they went upriver and wanted to go under the low bridges, they folded the stack down, took the stanchions out and lowered the canopy over the steering position. That was before World War I.

My dad started here in Alberni Canal in 1910, running mail, supplies and passengers up and down the canal to the fishing camps: Kildonan and San Mateo and Ritherdon Bay. They went down as far as Tofino and Ucluelet.

Our towing started in 1935 when Franklin River was opened up. We started with a little thirty-six-horsepower tug that could hardly handle a few sections of shingle bolts, and eventually we wound up with twenty-one tugs. My uncle Percy and my dad were partners. Dad died in 1972, at which time I took the place over with my sister. We operated quite successfully until 1974, when she wanted me to buy her out. So I thought, what the heck, I've had forty-five years of working, I might as well go along with her. So we sold it in 1974.

Today, however, these owner-operators are in a much tougher position than that faced forty years ago by pioneers like Claude Thicke, Harold Jones, Harold Elworthy or Bill Dolmage. In the early days a man could buy a boat and perform just about every type of towing. Today, towing has become much more specialized. Logs are increasingly being transported by barges, which are getting bigger and bigger. And even if a new tug can be financed, the cost of the barges themselves, as they become larger and more specialized, is prohibitive.

An individual might succeed if he got a tug, ran it himself and avoided the union. His long hours of work would, in time, pay for equity in the boat. He might even be able to buy a second boat, if he had a son or daughter to run it who was also willing to put in years of long days. Beyond that, he would have a very difficult time, not simply because of the financing entailed, but because the volume of work necessary to sustain such expansion would quite likely attract stiff competition from a larger and better-financed operation. The problems, nevertheless, do not seem to be discouraging people from entering the business.

An aspect of the towboating industry, which was and still is characteristic, is the family company or the participation of sons and grandsons of tugboat men. A third generation of Cosulichs works at RivTow, and a grandson of one of the original Stone brothers works on the tugs out of Port Alberni. Two of Bill Dolmage's sons are in the business with single-boat operations: John started a second Dolmage Towing Company, and Bill has a company called Hatoco Marine Services. Russ Cooper, a grandson of Thomas Cooper, still manages Westminster Tug Boats. The Warren family, descendants of James Warren, master of the *Beaver* and one of the province's first towboaters, still operates a couple of small tugs around Sooke and Victoria. There are probably many other second- and third-generation people in the industry today.

The size and scale of the towboat industry is revealed in the statistics. The current annual revenue is approximately $200 million. Seaspan, with about fifty tugs, accounts for close to thirty-five per cent of this income. RivTow, with about eighty-five boats (including those of its subsidiaries, half of which are under 40 feet long), takes twenty-eight per cent. The forest company towing affiliates, with a combined fleet of about thirty boats, take another twenty-five per cent. This leaves twelve per cent for everybody else. Expressed differently, something in the order of ninety-five per cent of the business is conducted by twenty-two members of the Council of Marine Carriers, which took over most of the functions of the B.C. Towboat Owners' Association in 1974.

The statistics tell one part of the story. There are other ways of looking at the industry that tell even more. It is hard to imagine, for example, two companies more different in character than the two that dominate the towing business in B.C., Seaspan and RivTow. They both were created from diverse companies, people and tugboats reaching far into the industry's past. The key people in each company, Jim Byrn at Genstar Marine and Cecil Cosulich at RivTow, are probably the only people in the business who grew up on and around towboats and also went to university.

RivTow gives one the impression that it is, perhaps, the biggest gyppo operation on the coast. Although there is nothing seedy or rundown about it, RivTow is in many ways casual and informal, taking the same kind of haphazard approach to appearances found in a hard-working, money-making independent coastal logging camp. Essentially, RivTow is a conglomeration of a number of small companies, some of which did not give up their independence willingly. Much of the company's drive comes from independent towboaters who decided to throw in their lot with RivTow rather than fight a losing battle against rising costs, multinational forest companies and lack of finances. Some of the companies that are a part of RivTow have kept their own names, such as Bute Towing and Westminster Tug Boats. There is a consciously maintained family atmosphere, and there is a feeling that the real heart of the company still lies in the battered little 30-foot river boats herding booms of logs down the Fraser. There is also a feeling that if you owned a towboat and had some business that RivTow wanted, you would not stand a chance.

Seaspan, on the other hand, is primarily a melding of large, successful companies. It has a cosmopolitan atmosphere about its operations that reflects both the nineteenth-century urbanity of Victoria and the tough modernity of Vancouver. These conflicting elements perhaps account for the tension that also seems inherent in the company. Seaspan boats tend to be immaculate. There is a sense of cool professionalism, a pride in being part of number one—combined with an undercurrent of frustration at the compartmentalized, bureaucratic corporate structure that marks Seaspan as a multinational operation.

Undoubtedly these two companies will continue to dominate the industry for a long time; their ability to finance the equipment required by their chief customers, the forest companies, will ensure that. The direction in which each will go—the types of work in which they will specialize, the areas into which they will expand—is open to speculation, as is the future of the entire industry. Both companies are already engaged in some U.S. west coast and deep-sea towing, and no one else in the business today is likely to enter that costly field, apart from the limited barging down the west coast of the United States performed by Kingcome Navigation for MacMillan Bloedel. And both companies are already working in the Arctic, which promises to become a major towboating part of the world. The best route into the Arctic is down the Mackenzie River, which is ice-free for a much longer period each year than is the alternate route through the Bering Sea. The Mackenzie and the shallow inshore waters of the Arctic Ocean are much more suited to a tug-and-barge mode of transportation than to ships.

Some of the factors that will determine the extent to which the B.C. towboat industry becomes involved in the Arctic are political. One factor is the Jones Act in the United States, which presently restricts the transportation of goods between two U.S. ports to American vessels. If this law were repealed or amended, no doubt a vast amount of material would move between the North Slope of Alaska and the continental United States via the Mackenzie River. A second factor is the extent to which the Canadian government will encourage or allow private companies to operate in the Arctic. The present attitude seems to view this part of Canada as a federal fiefdom to be developed by Crown corporations. When this situation changes, as it undoubtedly will, possibly a wide variety of towboat operations will evolve, not all of them necessarily controlled by Seaspan or RivTow.

In British Columbia, the future of water transportation by tug and barge seems assured. For environmental reasons the forest companies are beginning to sort and bundle their logs on dry land. This practice will become more common as they begin logging more second-growth timber, which is smaller than the trees cut in the past and, therefore, easier to handle on barges. It is possible that, as the forest companies begin thinning their second-growth stands and utilizing a lot of what is now considered waste, they will convert this wood to chips at the site and barge it to pulp mills. If that happens, there will be a large increase in the demand for barges of all sizes, along with the appropriate tugs to tow them.

Rising fuel prices will have an effect on the future of the towboat industry. Already, some people have proposed a return to the more fuel-efficient, slow-speed diesel engines of the sort used in the 1920s and '30s. Some companies are now telling their masters to slow down their engines in order to save fuel. Such practices may reintroduce at least a touch of the leisurely pace that was once an enjoyable feature of towing. The fuel crisis has also brought back a few sailing ships, though they are nothing like the old barques, brigs and clipper ships that once sailed up to Cape Flattery. These modern ships have sails controlled by computers and electric motors. If they prove to be efficient and economical, it is conceivable that tugs will once again

125. The *Kitmano* breaking ice in Kildala Arm, December 1971. The 47-foot, 700-horsepower tug was built in 1955 by Allied for Capt. Bill Cogswell, and is now owned by RivTow.

go out off Tatoosh to meet and escort sailing ships through Juan de Fuca Strait and the tricky waters of the Strait of Georgia and Puget Sound.

125

9 / *Life on the Boats*

Any description of what life was like in the early days of wood-fired steam tugs is based largely on informed guesswork. The boats are long gone, as are most of the people who worked on them. There are, however, a few pictures and a few hints in letters and other written accounts. To have worked on the *Beaver*, for example, would have meant just that—work. Hard work. Reportedly she burned seven to nine cords of wood a day, and a cord of wood is eight feet long, four feet high and four feet wide. The duties of almost all her many crew members would have been concerned with firewood; finding, cutting, loading and stowing it, and keeping an endless flow of it moving into the firebox. An experienced seaman was far more likely to sign on a sealing schooner, one of the tall ships or, at worst, one of the stern-wheelers on a regular run in and around the mouth of the Fraser. The crew of a tugboat were a mixed lot, and most of them appear to have gone on to find employment outside the young towing industry.

Whenever a wood-fired steam tug had to make a long trip—to the head of Loughborough Inlet, for instance—she would have to take along about a dozen extra men to cut wood. At some midway point, perhaps at Desolation Sound or Shoal Bay, the woodcutting gang would be dropped off to cut and stack huge amounts of wood on the beach, above the high-tide mark, and the tug would carry on. The master had to work the tides right and time the trip well in order to get back before the wood on board ran out. Otherwise, the crew would have to row into a beach, chop down trees, buck them into lengths and haul the wood out to

the boat.

The wood-burning steamers were, mercifully, not around for long. Soon, most tugs were fired with coal, which turned out to be a mixed blessing. To fuel, the boat merely pulled in under the tipple at Union Bay or Nanaimo, the gate was opened and the coal thundered down the chutes into the bunkers. Coal had advantages over wood, but it was dusty and dirty, and still involved a great deal of hard physical labour. Large coal-fired tugs like the *Lorne* still carried a crew of thirteen.

The hierarchy on board a boat is very well defined: master, mate, engineer, fireman, cook and deck hand. The master, skipper or captain of a tug is usually called the "Old Man" by the crew. Masters call each other "Cap." By maritime tradition, the master's word is law. He makes the final decisions, such as whether to chance the weather and tide or to hole up for a day of waiting that might stretch into a week or two. On an oceangoing ship the master usually stays out of sight, makes his rounds and is there when needed. On a tug, however, the master takes his turn on watch and takes the wheel in a tight spot or to relieve someone else. If he is a good captain, he maintains his boat well, drives his men hard and teaches them everything he knows.

He was, and still is today, never really off duty: legally, morally and historically, the master bears the burden of responsibility for the life of his crew and the

126

126. The *Sea Giant* (Dolmage Towing) and three of her crew of seven taking a break, sometime in the 1950s.

safety of his vessel. It takes a certain kind of person to accept this responsibility, one who is also wise enough to refrain from rushing into the wheelhouse every time the course is altered or the engines are slowed, especially in the dead of night while beating across Hecate Strait in a full gale with a green mate on watch.

The master's quarters were usually a private cabin directly behind the wheelhouse. (The captain of the *Lorne* enjoyed the luxury of a private bathroom, but most did not.) The way he spent his time off, shut away in his quarters, was often a matter of wild speculation on the part of the crew. Some captains slept, some drank and some built model ships or wrote poetry. Every one of them had all his senses tuned to

the boat, alert to every change in engine speed and compass course.

In the old days, there was the occasional skipper who arranged for the mate to be on watch when the tug left Vancouver, bound for coal at Nanaimo before going up to Rock Bay for a log boom. On these trips the skipper would be accompanied on board by a lady friend, who disappeared into his quarters with him; she would disembark at Nanaimo and go back to Vancouver on the ferry.

The mate is someone who is in training to be a captain. On a tug, he shares watches with the master: six hours on and six off. He is responsible for every detail of keeping a vessel running and doing its job,

127

127. Capt. Ernie Landheim at the wheel of the *St. Faith*, 1926.

Claude Thicke
Former president, Blue Band Navigation

Billy McNeil was a real tugboat skipper. He took his chances and he won nearly every time. He'd be tied up there at Trail Island waiting for the weather, and all the tugs tied there would get together at one place. And he'd say, "I'm going over for coal."

Somebody would say, "You'll miss the weather."

But he'd go and get back and, when the weather got good, he'd have enough coal to make it to Vancouver and they wouldn't.

He took the *Pronative* into Porpoise Bay to get a boom of logs once. He had to come out through the Skookumchuck and down past Sechelt. He passed these four tugs tied up at Trail Island and somebody there said, "There's one fellow that's going to lose his boom." Next thing they saw was the *Pronative* coming back. He went by them and in behind Sechelt again, picked up another tow, and came out and passed them. He did that four times while they were tied up not doing anything.

He took the chance, or at least he knew the weather better than they did. He treated the fellows decently, but he could treat them roughly too. You did what he said or you'd go back with a broken jaw or something. He was skipper always.

Mickey Balatti
Retired towboat captain

The old steam tugs of years ago, the wooden boats, had small power. At the time they thought they were powerful, but they weren't. When they started to make steel hulls, they loaded them up with power. They made them beamy so they could put these big, wide diesel engines in them. These engines were heavy so they put them way down low in the water and then they weren't sea boats anymore.

They all wanted to put more power in so the tug could tow more and make more money, with less crew. At that time everything was so new that even the guild and the government weren't after them to man the boats properly.

When I was mate there'd be one deck hand, and no man on your watch. You might work from six to twelve. You'd get no sleep on your off watch, come back on watch at twelve and be headed someplace running light. You hadn't had any sleep for eighteen hours and it was very, very hard to stay awake by yourself. You know you've got to stay awake because everybody's sleeping. If you put her up, boy, you drown the whole works.

The engineer would be in the engine room, and if there was a good second engineer sometimes he'd come up with a cup of coffee for you. It wasn't right, you know. Later the government ruled that there should be two men on watch at all times.

If you're in fog or traffic, or some damn thing, you got to keep a lookout, and you got to steer the boat, you got to navigate properly. One man can't always do this. If you got into problems like that you'd call the skipper. Some of those old skippers were pretty good and would jump right up. And some, if you called them at night, would bawl the hell out of you.

There were a lot of things to contend with. I don't know if it was better in those days or now.

from tying up the tow to fixing the plumbing; as much as possible, he delegates these tasks to deck hands. His position is similar to that of a foreman. The mate is responsible for every deed and misdeed of the crew, yet has the often thankless job of implementing the captain's decisions—most of which he has resolved to do differently when he has his own command. One of the few benefits of his job, at least on a large old tug like the *Lorne*, was a main deck cabin, which he might have to share if there were a second mate or other officer.

The engineer is always known as the "Chief." The name is left over from the days when there were at least two engineers on a boat, one of them a chief engineer. The engineer stands a little outside the ship's hierarchy. The captain does not issue orders to the Chief; he consults with him and makes requests for things such as more speed. The engineer is a man apart; outside the engine room he always seems slightly detached, partly because he is listening to the engine, but mostly because he considers anything going on outside his domain to be irrelevant. For an engineer, the primary function of a boat is to provide flotation for the engine, and any other activity in which the boat engages, such as towing logs, is incidental.

On the old tugs with steam or with slow-speed semi-diesel engines, two engineers were needed, for these types of engines required constant adjustment, tuning and general tinkering. Today, with high-speed diesel engines, most tugs carry only one engineer; and tugs that work around a harbour or close to home do not have an engineer. Some owners and managers believe that all engineers on tugs could be dispensed with entirely; they suggest that engine problems could be dealt with by crew members if a shore-based engineer gave instructions over the radio. This kind of thinking makes engineers melancholy and captains nervous. The last thing that a captain wants to do is work on a cranky engine with a monkey wrench during a gale.

The job of fireman on a coal-fired tug demanded a lot of hard physical labour. He had two jobs: shovelling coal—perhaps five tons a day on a tug the size of the *Lorne*—and disposing of the ashes. The engine room was not very noisy; there was only the rhythmic sound of shovel against coal, the hiss of imperfectly adjusted

steam valves and connections, and the low roar of the fire. The problem was the coal dust and the heat. In the winter the engine room might be comfortably warm, but in summer it was unbearably hot. The fireman's life was devoted to the task of keeping up a good head of steam in the boilers and his primary interest was the reading on the pressure gauges; what was tied to the end of the towline and where the boat was going were of little concern. On the *Lorne*, the two firemen and two engineers shared quarters below decks, aft of the engine room. Firemen were employed on tugs until the switch to oil and diesel engines eliminated their jobs. The bunks were then assigned to the wireless operators who were beginning to work on some of the big tugs.

Towboat cooks come in two varieties: full- and part-time. The cook has to tread a fine line between the amount of money the owners are willing to spend on food and the judgement of the crew. All cooks, however, who work on boats or in logging camps produce the same basic food—meat and potatoes. This is not because they cannot produce exotic dishes, but because the same meal has to satisfy the varying tastes of many hungry men. The good cook can work within these restrictions and still come up with a meal that produces a satisfied belch from the mate and a few minutes of amiable conversation over coffee and dessert.

Most cooks on the big old tugs were Chinese. On the smaller boats, a cook doubled as a deck hand; in practice this involved constant running in and out of the galley to secure a line, put the potatoes on to boil, take a turn at the wheel, check the roast, pump the bilges, keep a close eye on the Old Man's face when he tasted his dinner, and always, always keep the coffeepot full.

The cook's job is the only job on board a tug that is sometimes filled by a woman. The towboating industry was and remains a male-dominated industry. This is not because women are unable to perform the tasks involved in towboating: over the years a number of them have worked with their husbands on owner-operated boats. Company-owned tugs, however, have limited the role of women to that of cooks, and even that is rare. The explanation offered for this situation is that a tug is a very small vessel having a tight social

Ed Taylor

Retired towboat captain and dispatcher

I quit Vancouver Tug and got a job with Cliff Towing on the *Wilmurdell*. She's a coal burner. I'm up at the wheel, coming down out of the narrows, and the skipper's there with me. I'm decking and the chief engineer's standing there on the bow waving. I says, "What does he want?"

"Oh," says the skipper, "I guess he wants to dump the ashes now that we're out of the narrows."

"Okay," I says, "I'll give him a hand." So I run down there and he's got a great big steel bucket this high and a chain and block to pull it up out of the boiler room. I dump several of these alongside and when it's all over I head back up to the wheel.

The engineer says, "Where the hell are you going?"

"Back up to the wheel," I says.

He says, "No you're not, you're going to start trimming."

Down each side is a bunker. There's ports all along the deck, four on each side, where they dump the coal in. You get down in there with a little shovel and a little lantern and start heaving the coal towards the end of the bunker, then end up with a scoop shovel.

We get over to Cowichan Bay where we have to make up our own boom. The mate says, "You're mine now." We put the work boat over the side and make up the booms, section after section. We were there a whole week. Besides shovelling coal and working on the boom, you got a night off to sleep. That's all you did was sleep, you were so damn tired. I lost fifteen pounds in two weeks.

Finally the boom was made up, over fifty sections. Now we're going to Vancouver. There were eight tugs on that tow and the boom's four sections wide, the limit you could get through Porlier Pass. We hung on the other side of that pass for a week waiting for weather to calm down in the gulf because it's a long shot across to that North Arm or Howe Sound.

Anyway, away we go up into Howe Sound. All these tugs start breaking out different booms, some going to Port Moody, some up the river and others to Centre Bay where Cliff had his booming ground. We end up with a string for Iona Island. We let all those boom chains go, and all those wires, and God knows what that we had strung out all over that boom to save it in case we got in a blow.

We get all that work done, shovel more coal and get that boom tied up at Iona Island. Then the skipper says, "Ed, you got the night off."

It's about midnight. Isn't that great. I got the night off.

He says, "We'll be taking on fifteen tons of coal at eight tomorrow morning."

And I says, "Cap, good-bye." I got right off that boat with my suitcase and I'm gone. Jeez, I never quit a job so quick in my life.

Later I got my master's ticket and was the skipper of a little tug, the *La Fille*, with a three-man—later four-man—crew. Then I got on up the ladder to bigger tugs with up to eight-man crews. Then I moved into the office, dispatching, and was eighteen years ashore. In 1971 I retired and I've never looked back.

Ed Taylor

Retired towboat captain and dispatcher

When jobs were tight during the Depression, this guy quit his job on a tug, so I jumped into it. It was a three-man boat so I was cook, second engineer, deck hand and mate. It was only a little boat and we were on this run with Home Oil products. There were about forty-odd stops all over the coast—you start in Howe Sound and end up in Alert Bay or Port McNeil. You went up all through the backwoods country. You'd be away ten days to two weeks on that run.

The problem is when I'm on watch. The skipper's asleep, the engineer's asleep and there's just three of us. And I've got to cook—breakfast, dinner and supper. There's a hatch forward of the wheelhouse where the galley is, down below. I hook the doors open and jump down through that hatch, then nip back up because I'm weaving away somewhere, get her back on course again, peel the spuds, put the roast in the oven. I'm jumping up and down out of that hatch all the time getting things done.

One day the skipper came down there and I had everything on the table, the spuds, the carrots and the roast. It was one of those gate-leg tables, you lift it up and put a stick under it. He comes in and kicks the stick out and the food goes down onto the deck into the butts and dirt and fuzz.

I says, "Oh, Cap, look what you've done."

He says, "Look, I've got mine." He'd filled his plate. "Scoop it all up and wash it. Chris don't know, he's asleep."

So I cleaned it all up and Chris sat there chomping it all up and never knew the difference.

Lloyd Sias

Former towboat captain;
master, Port McNeil-Alert Bay ferry

Back then, being away three to four months at a time was normal. Some of us used to go out for longer than that. I can remember when we got a union agreement for half a day off for a week out, and we thought we were in heaven. Then we started getting one day off a week, and then we went to two or three days for every week out. Boy, we thought this was really something.

But my personal feelings are that we had more them days than we have today. What we had we appreciated. We were thankful for what we had. Today so many of these things that we thought were luxury, today they got to have it.

The thing that bothers me today—and it's not that I'm against unions, I'm a strong union man—is that the union agreement says that if he's a deck hand he can't cook or he can't wash paint or whatever.

You know, in yonder years when we brought a vessel into the dock it literally shone, whether it was winter or summer or what. The brass was all polished, all the paint was scrubbed down. It literally shone.

Them days some skippers were on the ship for practically the life of the ship, that was their ship. Years and years and years, you thought he was part of that ship. I had the feeling that that was my vessel, I owned part of it. You really took pride in it.

Today that seems to be lacking where you have two or three crews for a boat. I realize times have changed, but it has sure changed a lot of things that I guess some of us don't want to change with.

Drydie Jones
Retired towboat captain

Barney Johnson, Sr., was with the Grand Trunk Pacific for years. Then he was on the old *Prince Rupert* when it started. He was a daredevil. He was no fool, but he used to take a hell of a chance sometimes.

He'd be tied up at the CPR dock here in Victoria and a lot of skippers wouldn't go out if it was foggy, but he'd always go out. I wondered how in Sam Hill did he know how long to back out, how long to go astern and when to go ahead to go out the harbour. You can only back so far from the CPR dock, or you'll wind up against the Johnson Street bridge.

So I asked him, and he said, "That's easy enough if you're a good skipper. All you have to do is get the second mate or the chief to watch the clock every time you leave the dock. And then you ask him, 'How long before I went ahead?' And you keep track of that every time. When it gets foggy, there it is in black and white."

On the *Rupert* he had a chief officer, Neil Grey, with him. They were coming down Grenville Channel, and it's very deep along there. You can go right along the damn beach and you won't hit nothing, it goes straight down.

He was coming down there at eighteen knots in thick fog, and the whistle was set to go off every minute or two. One man went out one way on the bridge, and one the other. Barney was at the speaking tube going down from the bridge to the wheelhouse. If one echo came back before the other, he'd yell down to go two or three degrees to port or starboard. Well, old Grey was over on the starboard side of the bridge, kind of leaning out and—zip—he lost his cap over the side. "You crazy fool!" he yelled. "I lost my hat! A branch hit it."

"You're crazy," the captain said, "the wind blew it off."

"There's no wind," Grey said. "A branch hit it. I know, I heard it snap."

So the captain hollered down the tube, "Port five degrees!"

When they got down to Vancouver, Grey quit. Said the captain was nuts. When the fog cleared and Grey was off watch, he'd gone up and looked and, by God, there was a fir branch sitting underneath the lifeboat.

Bill Dolmage
Former president, Dolmage Towing; retired manager, Kingcome Navigation

Working on the pilchards on the west coast of Vancouver Island, we were forty miles offshore. The trouble was that we were towing scows—small scows, but scows. At nighttime the seine boats could drift, but we couldn't, because if there was no wind the scow would come up on top of us. So we had to go slow all night long. We were running twenty-four hours a day when we were out there; it was too hard work.

It wasn't good either, because forty miles is eight hours offshore, much too far for a thirty-two-foot boat. And with the fog you never knew where you were half the time. All you could do was head north, and you knew you'd hit Vancouver Island somewhere. If it was really thick, you'd put your head outside of the wheelhouse and listen for breakers. If you could hear breakers you knew it was too close and you could swing out. Then you wouldn't know if you were east or west of, say, Sydney Inlet, unless you picked up Estevan lighthouse.

It was too far out, so after a while they didn't use scows any more, they used packers. But when I was there we were going into Sydney Inlet and Matilda Creek, where the Gibson brothers were. I worked there until the middle of October, and then we took the scows and headed for Barkley Sound. Well, October can be a pretty dirty month on the west coast. We had to pick our weather, that's for sure.

We tended for herring in Barkley Sound until February fifth—they stopped fishing when they began to get the roe. Now they start fishing on February fifth. They want the roe.

order, and the presence of women crew members would produce discord on board. And, the argument continues, though a woman might be able to work successfully in this traditionally male environment, the wives at home would not tolerate it.

The position of deck hand on a coal-fired steam tug had to be one of the least desirable jobs. After casting off the lines at the coal dock, he was usually sent below with a short-handled shovel; crawling on his hands and knees, he trimmed the bunkers so as to balance the boat. He spent a lot of time in those coal bunkers; as the coal nearest the firebox was shovelled in by a fireman, it had to be replaced with coal that was farther back in the bunkers. Then the deck hand helped the fireman to dump the ashes, after which he hosed down the decks before going off watch. His quarters were in the forecastle, located below decks in the bow, and he shared them with the other deck hands. A dim light filtered into this space through a porthole or two, or a skylight. If the decks leaked, as they did on some poorly maintained boats, the coal dust from the decks washed through, adding damp and grime to the discomfort of bedbugs. An additonal disadvantage of the forecastle is its location in the bow, which subjects it to the maximum effects of a rough sea.

In those days the men and the occasional women who worked on the towboats spent most of their lives on board. It was more a way of life than a job, for a

128. Tugs tied up for Christmas at the Hind Bros. wharf, with mast-top trees, 1945.

trip might take four or five weeks. Family life was a difficult proposition; a towboater's wife rarely saw him and his children hardly knew him. With luck, a tug would tie up in town overnight and the crew could go home to their families, but next morning the tug would leave on another long trip. It was not much different, in that respect, from working on a fish boat or in a logging camp. The pressures to take a shore job were great, but in spite of the drawbacks, the best of the young men went on to become mates and skippers and spent their working lives on the boats. The pay? A captain earned $100 a month, the engineer a bit less and the crew $30 a month each.

Each tugboat company had a character of its own.

At Kingcome Navigation the money was good and the boats were well built and maintained. However, making the same runs over and over to Powell River from the various logging camps could become boring.

M.R. Cliff was known as a hard man to work for. His crews got little time off since he did not like to see his boats tied up at the wharf not making money. He used to prowl the back roads along the Fraser in an old Rolls Royce—its back seat and trunk filled with spare boom chains, shovels, axes and anything else he thought might be needed—checking up on his boats and crews. He would also park on one of the bridges waiting for a boat to come in from the north with a tow. While the tug was passing under the bridge, he lowered a basket

129

129. The *Charles H. Cates IX* (ex-*Moonlight*) and two of her crew in a restful moment. The tug was built in Vancouver in 1912.

of food and other supplies for the next trip, so that the crew could head right back out again. He always supplied the materials to keep his boats in good repair; their paint was new and their brass shone. In spite of the drawbacks, M.R. Cliff was a good company to work for, and few people ever left it to work elsewhere.

Pacific Coyle, on the other hand, was known as a tightfisted outfit that spent little on upkeep and less on wages. Once, so the story goes, the company had chartered out the *Lorne* to the Gibson brothers to tow log barges from the Queen Charlottes. A day or two before Christmas the whole towboat fleet traditionally came into Vancouver, spent the holiday ashore and headed out on Boxing Day. The crew of the *Lorne* had just come into the Coyle wharf and were up at the office collecting their pay when Gordon Gibson walked in. He pointed out to E.J. Coyle that he had chartered the *Lorne* for a full year; since his logging operation was shut down until after New Year's Day, he insisted that the tug be left at the wharf and the crew be given the same time off. This was unheard of; Coyle was astounded. Then Gibson handed the mate, Drydie Jones, a big envelope. Drydie and the crew went back down to the tug to open it: inside was an envelope for each crew member, and inside each envelope was a $100 bill.

The introduction of diesel engines and the switch from flat booms to rafts and log barges had a large

130

130. Tying lines from the *Island Commander* to the log barge *Island Hemlock* circa 1956. Both vessels were owned by Island Tug & Barge.

131. RivTow employees tying lines from a tug to a barge, 1979.

132. A RivTow worker making fast a chain from inside a side boomstick to a swifter, to prevent loss
of logs from the head corners of a flat boom tow.

impact on the nature of the job. Tugs no longer had to run over to Nanaimo or Union Bay for a load of coal before they could head north. A diesel engine could be started in a few minutes, instead of hours, to take advantage of a lull in the weather. The pace began to quicken because the boat was always ready to go and also because rafts and barges could be towed in open waters and withstand more weather than booms. Tugs spent less time tied up waiting for weather and the crew had fewer opportunities to throw a fishing line over the side.

Not only were the diesel engines quicker starting, more efficient and cheaper to operate, but they also could be run with a smaller crew. By 1925, it was

133

possible for an independent operator to buy a rather small but powerful tugboat and operate it alone or with a deck hand or two. However, the crews still spent long stints at sea and the bulk of the work was the same: nudging forward the river of logs that flows south along the coast into the mills on the lower mainland and Vancouver Island.

The Depression of the 1930s also played a hand in transforming working conditions. The key to a company's survival was to run a lean operation, and the crews, in order to keep their jobs, were willing to work for less money. When World War II came along there was more work, but both wages and towing rates were frozen. The belt-tightening period lasted about fifteen years. After the war, wages and working conditions began to improve steadily. In 1951 a master earned about $230 a month, while deck hands still received less than $100. In 1954, the practice of granting three days off after six 24-hour work days was instituted. In 1958, deck hands were earning $300 a month; overtime and paid holidays were added for all workers in 1963.

In the late 1950s and early 1960s, a new type of tug began coming off the ways in boatyards. The new tug was all steel—even the wheelhouse, galley and living quarters—and had a lot more power packed into it, 1,400 to 2,000 horsepower. It was designed to carry smaller crews of four, five and sometimes six men. The crews worked long hours in these all-steel boats that vibrated and resonated to the high-pitched whine of their 1,800-rpm diesel engines. Working on some of these tugs was not pleasant, not only because of the noisy conditions or the acrimonious relations between the unions and the companies, but also because of the dangers involved. A number of tugs had gone down in B.C. waters with a loss of many lives. The crews and unions blamed the shipyards for building poor boats and the owners for undermanning them. The owners blamed the crews for poor seamanship and for failing to observe safety measures. Fortunately, out of this situation grew a concerned attitude towards safety on the part of everyone involved in the industry, and much of the hazard of working on tugs was removed.

Over the same period great improvements were made in the living conditions on board tugs. The unions demanded and in the end received a private cabin for each crew member, all above the water line.

133. Inside the mess room of Pacific Towing Service's *Pacific Force*, built in 1980.

Compared to most of the older tugs, these are luxurious quarters. Each cabin has a wash basin, a comfortable bed and clean linen. Washers and dryers have replaced the old-time bucket and the clothesline strung across the afterdeck. The galleys are equipped with every modern appliance imaginable, including a television set. The entire superstructure has been encased in antivibration materials and sound-deadening devices to the point where in some tugs, so the owners claim, you have to look at the gauges to tell if the engines are running.

The contracts negotiated in 1976 gave captains about $20,000 a year, mates and engineers slightly less. Deck hands received about $13,000. Time off was calculated on the basis of 1.24 days off for every day of two six-hour watches worked—in effect, a 37.5-hour work week. Crew members spent 144 to 150 days a year working and were given the rest of the time off.

The effect of all these changes in wages, living and working conditions, safety, and the capabilities of the boats themselves has been to create a fleet of perhaps three hundred towboats operating in a manner reminiscent of the "good old days" of the classic tugs like the *Sea Lion* which the old-timers remember with fondness and nostalgia.

Today, when a modern tug like the *Seaspan Cutlass* leaves the company wharf in North Vancouver to tow a 300-foot fuel barge to Prince Rupert, it is just as

134

134. The *Seaspan Cutlass*, owned by Seaspan.

much of an adventure as it was a century ago when the *Isabel* set out for Tatoosh to bring in a sailing ship. The *Cutlass* is an 82-foot tug with twin 900-horsepower Detroit diesels, built in 1974 for Seaspan at its subsidiary, Vancouver Shipyards. She carries a six-man crew—captain, engineer, mate, two deck hands and a cook—each with his own on-deck cabin. Her galley is spacious and comfortable. Her rubber-mounted engines can barely be heard in the wheelhouse, which has windows all around for maximum visibility and is crammed with the most up-to-date electronic gear available. In short, she is a thoroughly modern general-purpose tug capable of towing a loaded barge three times her length at a speed of eight to ten knots.

In spite of elaborate radio communications systems, once the *Cutlass* unties her lines the decisions are made by the captain. The barge is an hour late in loading and the tide is already running strongly through the Second Narrows. Should he wait five or six hours for the next tide, or chance it and risk colliding into the Second Narrows Bridge?

No one presumes to advise the Old Man on how to deal with the tide at the Second Narrows. He decides to sail her through and takes the wheel himself. Apart from the engineer, who is reading the paper, and the cook, who is cheerfully washing the dishes, the crew is on tense alert. The mate is keeping a searchlight on the barge so that he can see what it is doing, and the two deck hands are ready to jump into action if necessary.

Once into the tidal stream there is no turning back. The barge makes a few more wild sheers then settles down and follows along like an obedient dog as the Old Man opens up the throttle and the bridge is cleared safely.

The mate and one of the deck hands head for their bunks, the Chief makes a last check on his engines, while the Old Man and the other deck hand settle in for a long night's tow up the placid Strait of Georgia. Occasionally they radio the tug's position to Marine Traffic Control, which keeps track of all shipping in coastal waters. The deck hand fetches coffee from the galley and takes the wheel, while the Old Man charts their course and tries to figure out how to make up the lost time so that he can catch the slack tide at Seymour Narrows.

At midnight, the mate and the other deck hand appear to take their watch. The cook arrives in the galley at 5:00 A.M. to prepare breakfast for the Old Man before he takes over the 6:00 A.M watch. The mate goes off watch, eats breakfast and hangs around in the galley.

Tension is mounting a little because they have not regained the lost time and they are an hour late on a big ebb tide at the Seymours. Once again, what to do: spend six hours circling off Campbell River to keep the barge under control, or go on through? The Old Man decides to run Seymour Narrows and not lose more time. Coming into the narrows they shorten up on the towline to give them better control of the barge, which is already beginning to act up in the five-knot tide. It is just after dawn and past the point of no return when a fog settles in, so thick that the wheelhouse crew can barely make out the bow of the tug. The barge is out of sight, sheering wildly in the turbulent waters just off Maude Island.

The Old Man is taking a course as far to starboard as he dares, planning to run between Maude Island and the spot where Ripple Rock once stood. The radar indicates there are no other boats nearby, but an unspoken thought hangs heavy in the wheelhouse air. What if some fool is bucking his way through the narrows along the Maude Island shore, out of sight of the radar? If a boat is there the odds of crashing into it are very high.

As they round the point to Discovery Passage, the radar screen is still empty. The Old Man gives the last of his throttle and the *Cutlass* and her tow shoot through the narrows, heading north, pushed along by a two- or three-knot ebb tide all the way to Kelsey Bay. The only sign of nervousness that the Old Man has revealed is the ashtray full of butts that sits in front of him.

Throughout the passage of the narrows, the Chief has been finishing off his newspaper with a morning coffee, aware of what is happening but indifferent to the proceedings: as long as the engines keep running, it is none of his affair. The cook does not even know where they are and could not care less. His chief concern is what to serve for lunch.

When the sun breaks through the fog, the deck

hands and the mate busy themselves touching up some paint on the afterdeck, leaving the Old Man to his peace at the wheel. There is no need to talk about having shot the narrows in the fog. Although they have all made this trip dozens of times, they have learned something new this morning. And on a sunny day like this, working on a tug is the best bloody job in the whole world.

A couple of weeks later the Old Man will be in the Princess Mary Restaurant in Victoria for the weekly coffee meeting of working and retired towboat people. He will mention the trip through the Seymours in the fog, and the old skippers will shake their heads, some in disbelief, some in disapproval. ''You're daft. I'd never have tried that,'' one will observe. The Old Man will smile to himself because he knows full well that every one of them would have done the same thing if they had a tug like the *Cutlass*. For it is they who have taught him—first as a deck hand, then as a mate. The only difference is the sophistication of the boat he captains compared to those they sailed twenty years earlier.

Meanwhile, the *Cutlass* is proceeding on her journey, swinging wide around Chatham Point because Marine Traffic Control has warned of an approaching freighter. It is a perfect October day, not a cloud in the sky and a slight westerly kicking up a light chop. Off Walkem Islands, a school of porpoise appears alongside; they take turns riding the bow wave pushing out in front of the tug. There is little traffic, only the odd gillnetter heading south now that the fishing season is ended.

The day passes in slow, easy conversation. The Chief watches an afternoon quiz show on the television set in the galley, interrupted at one point by the two grinning deck hands who request his permission to use the engine room for the secret construction of a box that will enable the mate, who is a bit short, to see over the aft controls.

By the change of watch they have reached Alert Bay, where a stop is planned to pump off a few thousand gallons of fuel, an operation that will take several hours. When they pull into the harbour, a two- or three-knot tide is sweeping past the fuel dock. Fish boats are tied up all around, and it is going to be a tight squeeze to slide the barge in without doing any damage.

The Old Man orders the barge to be tied alongside and makes a pass at the dock, throwing the *Cutlass* into full reverse when he sees they will not make it. Scowling fishermen begin to appear on the decks of their boats, and the owner of the fuel dock, which is dwarfed by the barge, paces nervously, eyeing his new pilings. It takes three passes and half a pack of the Old Man's cigarettes before the barge is nudged in against the dock. The deck hands tie the lines and the mate goes to inspect a set of pilings that now lean at a crazy angle.

The Old Man shuts off the engines and heads to the galley for his supper. He is not in a good mood and is cheered only slightly when the mate reports that no pilings are broken and that a light tug with a towline will set them straight again. The Old Man is upset because the hour of manoeuvring that it took to dock, with all hands on deck, means that by the time the fuel is pumped off, by regulation the crew must be given a rest period. In the old days they would have untied and left when the unloading was finished, catching up on sleep as they travelled. Today the rules say that they must wait and sleep, and this irritates the Old Man, largely because the rules are beyond his control.

It is a warm, still evening on deck and the Chief gets out his fishing rod and makes a few tentative casts off the stern. The tug is tied up virtually in the centre of Alert Bay, which is strung out in a thin line along the shore.

The fuel is pumped, the obligatory rest period is observed and a low overcast dawn finds the *Cutlass* plowing through a light swell in the open waters of Queen Charlotte Sound. A storm is moving in, but before it builds to anything serious the tug and barge duck in behind Calvert Island to Fitz Hugh Sound, to begin the 250-mile haul through the narrow, protected waters of the inside passage to Prince Rupert.

Apart from the town of Bella Bella and the occasional lighthouse, the entire route is devoid of signs of civilization. There are no logging camps on this part of the coast because no use has been found for the stunted cedar and hemlock that cover the rugged, rocky coastline. It is a full day's sail through these twisting channels and passages to Prince Rupert. There is little to do except make position reports, watch the occasional boat go by and look out the rain-spattered wheelhouse windows. It is a tricky, narrow course that must have been a nightmare for the helmsman on an old steam tug, feeling his way along by the echo from his whistle and wrestling with a heavy wheel.

The chief hazard on a tug like the *Cutlass* is boredom. The Old Man and the mate fend it off on their respective watches by plotting meticulous courses in order to gain a minute here, another there, shaving time. They are easy, amiable watches, the Old Man granting occasional gifts from his hoard of knowledge: how to catch a back eddy around a certain point to gain a couple of minutes, when to shorten up on the towline, when to let it out. Some captains never pass this knowledge on, keeping it close to themselves in the little notebooks that they all carry. The Old Man does, though, and the crew likes him for this.

Near Bella Bella a new voice comes over the radio, speaking to traffic control. A RivTow tug and barge have come out of Ocean Falls, heading north, three or four miles ahead. "We'll catch him before Rupert," the Old Man says to the deck hand who is sharing his watch. He makes no move to use the power that he has in reserve; that would upset the Chief and, anyway, it would not be fair. He merely checks his courses a little more closely, shaving off seconds now instead of minutes.

Near midnight, part way up a rain-swept Tolmie Channel, a double blip appears on the edge of the radar screen. He is gaining, as he has known for some time by the other tug's reports to traffic control, but the two pinpoints of light that mark the tug and its tow on the radar give him a certain satisfaction. When the mate comes on watch a few minutes later, the Old Man points at the blips. The mate nods and takes the wheel, settling in for the night.

Dawn finds the tug well up Grenville Channel, a narrow forty-five-mile chute running straight as an arrow almost to Prince Rupert. Ahead, through the rain, is the stern of the empty log barge being towed by the other tug. By now a full gale is blowing up Hecate Strait, but it is almost flat calm in the channel behind the protection of Pitt Island. The Old Man gets up and has his breakfast, while chatting with the Chief and the cook about the weather, then takes a cup of coffee up to the wheelhouse. He is pleased to note the other tug and barge, right where he expected them to be, about half a mile ahead. After a brief exchange, the mate heads for his bunk and the Old Man settles down with his chart of Chatham Sound, which is where he has decided to overtake the other tug. There has been no verbal acknowledgement, either on board the *Cutlass* or by radio between the two tugs, that for the past fifteen hours a tugboat race has been going on. There is no need to discuss it; such races have been run for a hundred years. They help to relieve the monotony and keep everyone on their toes.

The Old Man is determined to get to Prince Rupert first, and when the two tugs break out of Grenville Channel and the other tug swings to the starboard to clear a small island, the Old Man gives the deck hand a course that takes the *Cutlass* to port. While lying awake in his bunk, he had figured it right. By the time they hit the open water off Smith Island, a full gale is blowing and great sheets of water are flying off the tops of the waves. This raises havoc with the other tug's empty log barge, but the loaded fuel barge behind the *Cutlass* plows solidly through the waves.

By the time he heads off watch at noon, the Old Man is half a mile ahead and his last act is to call the RivTow office in Prince Rupert asking for a tug to assist in docking the barge. He spends the next two hours in the galley, enjoying a leisurely lunch and watching a football game on the television set until they enter the harbour.

A little two-man harbour tug steams out to meet them, bouncing around in the rough water, her decks half awash. As she pulls alongside the *Cutlass*, the radio picks up a call from the RivTow tug, by now half an hour out, calling her Prince Rupert office for assistance with the log barge.

"Roger, Cap," answers the skipper of the harbour tug. "Be with you as soon as I've finished with the *Cutlass*."

The Old Man allows himself one small smile. Behind his back, the mate and a deck hand are grinning from ear to ear.

135. RivTow employees rigging towing equipment.

10 / *The Boats Themselves*

Boats have a mystique. Their appeal extends far beyond those who take them out to sea. And among those who work on the water, the focal point of conversation is always the boats. Some of this fascination is owing to the individuality of boats. Even sister ships—boats built to the same design and specifications—have differences. A somewhat romantic school credits boats with having personalities, near-human characteristics. Perhaps. But among working mariners, the prime consideration is always how well a boat performs: how she takes to a heavy sea, how she handles in a following sea, how reliable her engines are, how pleasing to the eye her lines are, and so on.

In this respect, towboaters are no different from other mariners. Their conversation always comes back to the tugs, and that is an endless subject. In the century and a half since the *Beaver* first put a towline on a ship, several thousand tugs have worked on the coast: some estimate as many as 5,000. Almost all have had more than one owner, and some have had several; they have been renamed, rebuilt and had their engines changed. Most towboat people have worked on many tugs, so there are numerous conversational possibilities.

The records about tugs, on the other hand, are very sparse. A certain amount can be gleaned from the office of the Registrar of Ships, where boats must be registered, and a few publications contain spotty accounts of towboating and tugs. The largest body of knowledge about tugs lies in the long oral tradition established by people who remember the facts, the stories, the legends, the boats and the characters, and who pass them on to younger generations.

The evolution of the towboat in the Pacific northwest has been going on for just over a century. The first boats used as tugs were steam-powered side-wheelers like the *Beaver*. Their hulls were basically those of a sailing ship. They were side-wheelers because that was the way boats were built then. In some respects they were not very good tugboats: the position of the side wheels well forward of the stern and the location of the rudder near the stern meant that when the towline was attached somewhere on the rear deck, the boat was very difficult to steer. Side-wheelers were common until about 1880.

During roughly the same period, steam-powered stern-wheelers were used on the Fraser River to haul freight and passengers and occasionally to tow. They worked well as freight boats on the river because their bows could be run up on a bank and a gangplank thrown ashore for loading and unloading, but as towboats they were useless. For the towline to clear the paddle wheel on the stern, the tow post had to be attached at a considerable height, usually on top of the housework. This arrangement was unfortunately ideal for capsizing a boat if the tow happened to sheer off or the boat turned too sharply.

The first boat built in British Columbia specifically for towing was the *Isabel*. Edward Stamp needed a tug to tow lumber ships between Cape Flattery and his sawmill in Burrard Inlet, so he ordered a boat from

136

136. Close-up view of the rope fenders on the bow of the *Charles H. Cates IX* circa 1920.

James Trahey, a Victoria builder. Although the *Isabel* was a tug, she did not look much different from other side-wheel steamers cruising Puget Sound and the lower Strait of Georgia. There is a dearth of information on the *Isabel*'s specifications, but it is known that she was 146 feet long, with a 24-foot beam and a 9-foot hold. She burned coal, cost $50,000 to build and was launched on 25 July 1866. Her first master was Capt. Thomas Pamphlet. Stamp operated the tug for four years before she went to Puget Sound to carry passengers and freight. Then she towed coal ships between Cape Flattery and the mines at Comox and Nanaimo before and after Robert Dunsmuir bought her in 1888. Eventually she was converted to a barge, probably hauling coal, lumber and building stones around Victoria, until she faded out of sight twenty years later.

The first steamboat to be built in Vancouver was a tug called the *Maggie*. She, too, was a side-wheeler, but at 72 feet long and with only 20 horsepower she was considerably smaller than most other tugs then in business. The *Maggie* was built in 1873 by Jeremiah Rogers—as legend has it, on a platform in front of the Granville Hotel. Rogers built the tug to tow logs from his camp in English Bay to the Hastings mill. This short-distance towing did not require a large tug, and it marks one of the first log-towing undertakings on the coast.

The McAllister brothers of Victoria built what was probably the last side-wheel tug in B.C., the *Alexander*. They wanted the most up-to-date tugboat on the coast to firmly establish themselves in the ship-towing business—almost the only towing work available at that time. In the spring of 1875 they went north to the Skeena River, where the best wood was to be found, and had her built at the village of Port Essington. In November, the *Alexander* was towed to Victoria by the Hudson's Bay Company's steamboat *Otter* to have coal-burning steam engines installed. The *Alexander* was an enormous boat, 180 feet long with a 27-foot beam, and cost $80,000, a large sum at the time. The startled residents of Victoria promptly dubbed her ''McAllisters' Folly,'' somewhat prophetically as it turned out: the brothers went bankrupt within five years. Under the McAllisters the tug went through a number of masters, including George

Marchant and James Warren. In 1880, Warren purchased her for Robert Dunsmuir, paying $15,000, to tow coal ships. In 1890 the *Alexander* was sold to T.P.H. Whitelaw, a well-known San Francisco salvage master; he removed her engines and wheels and rigged her as a four-masted sailing schooner. She was used briefly as a whaler, tied up for some time in Port Townsend, then sold in 1902 to Pacific Towage and Lighterage Company of Victoria for $1,000. Pacific Towage used her as a log barge (probably the first attempt at log barging in the province) to supply sawmills in Victoria with timber from Vancouver Island logging camps.

The Hudson's Bay Company had brought out the *Otter* from England in 1853, and she was the first propeller-driven steamboat on the coast. The next two tugs in B.C. having this new method of propulsion were the *Pilot* and the *Etta White*. The *Pilot* was built in 1871 in Portland, Oregon, and was 121 feet long with a 22-foot beam. She passed through several hands, including those of the B.C. Towing and Transportation Company, who paid $12,500 for her. Robert Dunsmuir bought the tug in 1885 to tow coal ships until 1895, when she was converted into a scow. As a scow, the *Pilot* figured in a disaster typical of the scow-towing business. She was being towed by the *Velos* to the Haddington Island quarries for a load of stone during construction of the Parliament Buildings in Victoria. It was March and a heavy southeaster was blowing, so Captain Anderson of the *Velos* decided to turn back just off Trial Island. While the tug was coming around, she broke a rudder chain, and the *Pilot* dragged the tug onto the rocks. Both vessels broke up and five men lost their lives.

The *Etta White* was built in 1870 in Freeport, Washington, by two American mariners, George White and Henry Smith. Smith brought the 93-foot tug to Vancouver and served as her master for the next twenty-three years, towing ships and moving log booms for Moodyville mill. She burned and sank at Swanson Bay in 1920.

The steam propeller drive was not, however, used in B.C.-built tugs for some time; there was no local engine works. By the late 1870s, the skilled machinists, mechanics and engineers who were essential to provide boilers and engines were beginning to settle in the province. Foremost among them was Joseph Spratt, born in England and trained as a machinist in San Francisco. He established the Albion Iron Works on San Juan Island in 1861 and in 1872 moved to Victoria, where he built a foundry. It quickly became the largest marine machine shop north of San Francisco, building boilers, engines and other hardware. He sold the operation in 1888 but, during the few years he was in business, succeeded in establishing a modern shipbuilding depot.

Up to this time, steamboats burned wood to heat their boilers. These boilers, like the one in the *Beaver*, were simply rectangular reservoirs of riveted plates sitting above fireboxes and had working pressures of less than five pounds. The engines were noncondensing —that is, instead of the steam being condensed after it passed through the cylinder, it was vented up the exhaust tube to help create the enormous draft necessary to keep the often green wood burning. The amount of wood required to keep the steam pressure up for a day was phenomenal.

When Spratt went into business in Victoria, coal was replacing wood and was being used in much more efficient boilers and engines. The type of boiler that Spratt built was called a "scotch" or fire-tube boiler. The fire was directed through a series of tubes, around which the water circulated. These boilers could develop a working pressure of 250 pounds or more. The engines were a triple-expansion condensing type. The steam passed through a series of three or four cylinders, the pressure being lower in each succeeding one. The steam was then run through pipes outside the hull, where it condensed back to water, and was returned to the boilers. The advantage of these new boilers and engines was they could generate and use substantially increased steam pressure, giving them more power in relation to their size. This made it possible to build smaller boats, since the engines did not take up as much space. These boilers and engines also used fuel more efficiently and were much quieter than the noncondensing engine in which the vented steam produced a loud roar.

One of the earliest boats built by Spratt was the *Leonora*, which was completed in 1876. At 57 feet in length she was even smaller than the *Maggie*. She had a 9-foot beam, a long deck cabin for passengers and a towing bit on top of the cabin. She was built for James

Van Bramer to carry passengers and to tow around the Moodyville mill. Over the next three years, Van Bramer had another boat of similar design built, the 51-foot *Senator*, to carry passengers. When Van Bramer left B.C. he sold both boats to Donald McPhaiden, who also bought the 76-foot *Skidegate* and formed the Burrard Inlet Towing Company with them. This eventually became the Union Steamship Company, probably the most famous passenger and freight service on the coast.

For a number of years the *Leonora* worked mainly in the protected waters of Burrard Inlet: towing ships from the ballast grounds to berths at the Hastings or Moodyville mill, towing lumber scows out to ships and towing scowloads of rock, sand and gravel for construction work in Vancouver. Just after the turn of the century she was sold to the Keefer family, who put her to work towing their scows of building stones and paving blocks, as well as the occasional log boom from the logging camps that had opened up near Powell River. The *Leonora* spent her remaining years in that area and farther north, passing from hand to hand among the coastal handlogging and gyppo logging operations around Port Harvey, Minstrel Island and Port Neville. She finally sank in 1919 at Boat Harbour on Cracroft Island.

The *Leonora* is significant because she was one of the first relatively small tugboats that in later years were to be found in large numbers around all the coastal harbours and logging camps. These and similar operations required boats that could tow scows and logs, carry passengers and a bit of freight, but which did not have to be large or powerful enough to tow in ships from Cape Flattery.

In 1889 two tugs that were to become legends were built in British Columbia. In many respects the *Lorne* and the *Active* were prototypes of an indigenous B.C. towboat fleet. They did not have passenger cabins like the *Isabel* and the *Leonora*, nor did they have holds for freight. The *Lorne* and the *Active* were built to tow, and nothing else. The Dunsmuir family had the *Lorne* made to tow coal ships; she was designed by San Francisco naval architect George Middlemas and built by Robert Laing, one of Victoria's first and foremost boatbuilders. Laing had been trained in Scotland and moved to Victoria about 1850. The *Lorne* was 150 feet long, had a 25-foot beam and drew 18 feet of water. Her scotch boilers and triple-expansion engine, manufactured at Albion Iron Works, developed 1,250 horsepower with 160 pounds of steam pressure. Hers was the first triple-expansion engine to be made in Canada. The propeller, 12 feet in diameter with four detachable blades, was also cast by Albion. The hull below the water line was sheathed with 1,337 sheets of heavy-gauge copper, several of which were torn off during launching. She had spacious quarters for a 17-man crew who, when gathered in the main salon, were privileged to gaze upon portraits of the entire Dunsmuir family. She cost $60,000.

The *Lorne* was capable of making 14 knots and her large bunkers held 150 tons of coal. The towing equipment consisted of a tow post, a huge manila hawser 16 inches in circumference, and a capstan near the stern on one side of the afterdeck to pull in the towline. She had a wooden rudder rigged to the wheel with a block and tackle apparatus. To bring her about took two men straining to their utmost and eighteen turns of the wheel. Charles Cates gave an account of being on her once in Burrard Inlet and beginning a turn close to the Vancouver shore by cranking her around, hard to port: although Burrard Inlet is two miles wide there, she had to be stopped and backed off to keep from running aground on the North Shore. Later she acquired steam-powered steering and towline winches. There are two versions of the fate of the *Lorne*. One has it that she was bought by Shaeffer-Haggert and scrapped at the yard of B.C. Marine Engineering and Shipbuilding. The other says that she was tied up at Gambier Island and eventually sank there.

While a boat like the *Lorne* reflected the needs of Victoria-based towboaters for a powerful ship-towing tug, there was a growing demand in Vancouver for a different type of tug to tow logs. At this time logging camps were opening up at scores of locations between Vancouver and the north end of Vancouver Island. The tug had to be big enough to run light up the inside waters in rough weather on the way to pick up a tow, or to cross the Strait of Georgia for coal. It also had to be fairly large just to carry the coal needed for the long trip from East Thurlow Island to Vancouver, and to have roomy quarters for a crew of seven to ten men on

a trip that might take from two to six weeks depending on the weather. The boat did not need a lot of power because log booms could be towed only at a speed of one or two knots, otherwise the logs would bounce out or the booms would break up. The *Active* represented the first serious attempt at designing a tug to meet these requirements.

The *Active* was 116 feet long with a 21-foot beam. The triple-expansion engines were built in New Westminster by Heeps and developed 55 nominal horsepower. Originally she was intended to tow only four or five sections of logs. In fact, one of her early masters was severely reprimanded for bringing in a ten-section boom. However, the tug performed well beyond expectations as towboaters became more experienced at towing logs. In 1900 she brought a twenty-section boom through the First Narrows and was met by crowds of cheering people and a hired band. Later, still with her original engines, she routinely towed fifty-section booms.

In addition to log towing, the *Active* was used by Hastings mill to haul equipment and supplies to up-coast logging camps. One early job of this sort was transporting the knocked-down parts of a small tug, the *Eagle*, to Quadra Island. A one-mile trail was cut up to Village Bay Lake, where the tug was assembled by a young engineer, Lloyd Gore. The *Eagle* was used to tow logs that had been skidded to the lake by oxen. Once bagged at the outlet of the lake, the logs were flumed down to the salt water where they were boomed and towed to Vancouver by the *Active*. This was one of the first of a number of similar towing and fluming operations carried out on coastal lakes, and many of these lakes contain the remains of small tugs like the *Eagle*.

The *Active* remained with Hastings mill and its successor, the Canadian Western Lumber Company, until 1946 when she was purchased by Sparkie New at Coastal Towing. He bought her along with the *Petrel* and the *Gleeful* for $65,000. Six years later the *Active* was rebuilt and an 800-horsepower Enterprise diesel engine installed. She also got new housework to accommodate a smaller crew of seven men. The cabins were equipped with electric heat and wash basins, and the modernized galley had freezers. In 1956, Capt. Aage Sonum was bringing the *Active* and a fifty-section boom through the Hole-in-the-Wall, a very narrow passage between Maurelle and Sonora islands, when the tug hit a reef. With assistance from some small boats that came to the rescue from nearby logging camps, the *Active* was pushed into Owen Bay where she sank. She was raised a few days later and towed to Vancouver, but was too badly damaged to repair; her engine was removed and she was towed to Galiano Island and abandoned on a beach.

Over the years a number of vessels, in turn, have had the distinction of being referred to as the oldest working tug on the coast. Since the demise of the *Active*, that title has belonged to an unassuming tug called the *Swan*. There have been several *Swans;* this one was built in 1888 at the head of Rivers Inlet by Bob Drainey, a cannery manager, and was used to tow fish boats in the inlet. The 55-foot boat sank in 1922, was raised, then was sold to Tom Kelly, a prominent spruce logger on the Queen Charlotte Islands. He used her to tow logs between his camps and the rafting sites, where logs were made into Davis rafts. Capt. Don Peck, an old-time north coast towboater, chartered the *Swan* for a while, then Bill Bennick used her to tow logs between Pitt Lake and the Fraser. In the early 1930s her steam engine was replaced by a diesel and she kept pretty much to the Fraser, partially burning near its mouth in 1953. Alf and Helen Talbot bought the *Swan* in 1966 for their logging operation and put in a new engine in 1968, as well as a new bowstem and a Kort nozzle. In 1980, someone attempted to steal her from the Mission wharf and sank her in 35 feet of water. The Talbots raised and repaired her, and the *Swan* is back at work towing on the river.

Another boat worth mentioning from this period is the *Beatrice*, built in 1891. At that time a large sealing fleet was operating out of Victoria, employing more than 3,000 people on about 125 sailing schooners. Leaving Victoria each year, they ranged across the North Pacific, through the Bering Sea and down the Siberian coast into the coastal waters of Japan, hunting fur seals.

The *Beatrice* was built in Vancouver and, at 70 feet, was a typical sealing schooner. Her only power was from her sails. On her first trip, under a Danish captain named Bjaerra, she was in a storm about 400 miles off the northern B.C. coast. The crew, in keeping with standard practice at the time, set the storm sails, lashed the wheel and retreated below, leaving the ship to take

Sparkie New
Retired president, Coastal Towing

The *Beatrice* was originally a sealing schooner and had only sail, no engines. The Goodwins put the steam in her when she became a tug. They were using her for towing the old railroad barge between Victoria and Port Mann, back in the twenties sometime. I chartered her from the Goodwins first, and then we finally bought her.

She had a little compound engine, with a Holander boiler. It was terrific, the same principal as the Yarrow boiler, which is very well known. This Holander was was designed and built in Vancouver and it was made, if you please, of ordinary hydraulic pipe. The pipes that connected the mud drums to the steam drum were ordinary one-inch water pipes, extra heavy. They were bent back and forth, thirty feet in each one. They were joined with couplings with right-hand and left-hand threads, so when they were turned it screwed them together. This was the boiler, and the furnace part was in among this nest of pipes. You could raise steam in about five minutes. It was fast.

The *Beatrice* had two hundred pounds working pressure and a compound engine to accept it. Compounds don't ordinarily accept pressures like that, you need a triple expansion job. What they did in this case was to bush the high pressure cylinder down to a much smaller diameter, and then they took the big expansion from that one to the low pressure cylinder. It worked fine, was very efficient.

This was the sort of thing they did in those days, they had lots of imagination. At one time we got it all salted up and I thought we'd lost it. Somebody came along with a chemical that was able to dissolve the salt in the tubes and we got her working again. It was the first one ever cured that way.

Then eventually we had a fire and burned the housework, so we wrote her off and sold the hull. The next thing I heard she was being re-engined with a Gardiner and that's what she's got now, I guess. Her name was changed to the *Arrawac Freighter*.

She was a beautiful little sea boat, actually quite amazing. And she was quite successful as a tug, quite efficient—of course that's the high pressure steam.

care of herself. A huge wave flipped her over, throwing the cabin boy overboard. A few moments later another wave threw her upright, hoisting the cabin boy aloft, unharmed.

In 1899, the *Beatrice* was laid up in Victoria and disappeared from the records for a while. At some point she was acquired by J.J. Goodwin, who converted her to a tug. He removed the sails, added a wheelhouse and installed a Bolinder boiler with a compound steam engine. During the 1920s she was used to tow a railcar barge between Victoria and Port Mann. In 1943 Sparkie New chartered and eventually bought her, operating her in Coastal Towing until 1958, when she caught fire at the wharf in Vancouver and lost her housework. The

Beatrice was sold to H. Clay, who rebuilt her as a coastal freighter powered by a Gardiner diesel and renamed her the *Arrawac Freighter*. She was later acquired by Joe Moyle and operated by Andy Dumyn as a fish packer out of Quatsino Sound. She still works in the fishing industry, packing salmon and herring. The *Beatrice* and the *Thomas Bayard*—restored by Sterling Shipyard for the Vancouver Maritime Museum—are the only sealers left of a fleet that for fifty years was the mainstay of Victoria's economy.

For many years the *Brunette* also laid claim to the title of oldest working tugboat on the coast, erroneously as it turned out. She was built in 1890 at the Brunette Sawmill in New Westminster by Wesley Peck,

137

137. The *Swan* as she appeared in 1922 after being salvaged at Kimsquit. At that time her owner was Bob Drainey.

grandfather of the early Skeena River tug master Don Peck. She was 61 feet long and equipped with a wood-fired John Doty steam engine. The *Brunette* was built to tow logs but, unlike the larger *Active* and other log towers of that size, she was intended to tow only around the mill or on short hauls; her first twenty years were spent shifting booms and moving lumber scows from mill to shipside. The tug was owned briefly by Smith and Dollar mills, which sold her to M.R. Cliff in 1917. She was Cliff's first boat, the beginning of one of the coast's most successful log-towing companies. He repowered her with a semi-diesel in 1934 and a full diesel in 1953. As a steam tug she had carried a six-man crew, but by then she was down to three: master,

mate and engineer. For at least twenty years of the time that Cliff owned her, the *Brunette* was skippered by "Simmy" Simpson, who once estimated that he had put a couple of million miles on her, most of them on the run between Howe Sound and the Fraser. There is a story that Simpson viewed the *Brunette* as a lucky talisman and cautioned Cliff never to sell her. Shortly after Cliff sold her, the company went bankrupt and Cliff died a year later in 1959.

The *Brunette* spent several years mostly tied up and out of work until Vic Di Castri bought her in 1963 and took her to Powell River. He installed a new 325-horsepower diesel engine, fixed up the hull and put her to work towing logs and scows, berthing ships

138

138. The *Swan* looking much improved in Pitt Lake, 1973. She is the oldest working tug on the B.C. coast, owned by Alf and Helen Talbot.

139. The *Beatrice* in her original form as a sealing
schooner.

141

140

140. The *Beatrice* converted into a tug circa 1945 when she was owned by Coastal Towing.

141. The *Robert Preston*, later renamed the *Johnstone Straits*.

142. The steam tug *Hopkins* on the ways on the beach at Hopkins Landing, 1909. Arthur Moscrop (*l.*) designed the boat for Capt. Gordon Hopkins (*r*).

143. The *Hopkins* with her hull finished, 1910.

144. The completed *Hopkins* tied up at Sooke, 1911.
The tug was purchased around 1925 by Island
Tug & Barge and renamed the *Island Rover*.

around the pulp mill and standing by for rescue work in the Strait of Georgia. Di Castri was diligent with her maintenance and she was still in good shape when he sold his business in 1975. On her first trip out with her new owner, she came in with a split hull. The engine was removed and the hull was sold for a dollar to be used as a barge on an oyster farm. But she sank before she could be put to work and now lies on the bottom near Lund.

In the 1890s, a young English immigrant named Alfred ("Andy") Wallace arrived in Vancouver bearing with him a reputation as a builder of fine fishing boats. He established a small boatyard in False Creek in 1894; starting with lifeboats, rowboats and small fish boats, he graduated to stern-wheelers and, eventually, tugs. Wallace and a number of other boatbuilders who came to the province at about the same time played a vital part in the continuing evolution of the coastal log-towing tug, the class of boat that was the mainstay of the towing industry until after the Second World War. What evolved was a tug 70 to 100 feet long, with a 20- to 25-foot beam. Usually it was equipped with scotch boilers and a triple-expansion steam engine, producing under 300 horsepower. After about 1905, the tugs were provided with a steam winch located on the aft deck; the winch had its own engine but got steam from the main boilers. The winches held steel towing cables which, in addition to being stronger than the old manila hawsers, could be much longer, allowing the tow to follow well back out of the propeller wash. The hull design was still fairly close to the standard sailing boat hull.

No place else in the world was log towing being conducted on such a large scale, or was this particular class of tug being built. The tugs built elsewhere, especially in Europe, tended to be either much larger, more powerful deep-sea tugs or smaller harbour tugs. Other boatbuilding centres were shifting from wood to steel construction, but the B.C. tugs were built of wood, which was in good supply and of the best quality. The Pacific northwest boatyards attracted many skilled builders of wooden boats and the tugs built in B.C. were noted for the quality of their workmanship. The boats built then were among the finest ever made in the northwest.

One of the first tugs that Andy Wallace built was

the *Progressive*, launched in 1905. She was 77 feet long with an 18-foot beam and powered by a 300-horsepower triple-expansion steam engine. She very soon wound up at the newly formed Kingcome Navigation, and in 1917 made a bit of history by towing the first Davis raft across Hecate Strait. For a long time she towed logs and paper scows between Powell River and Vancouver, along with the *Ivanhoe*.

The *Ivanhoe* was another tug built by Wallace, hull number 50 out of his yard in 1907. She was 99 feet long, 22 feet wide and had the same engine as the *Progressive*. Originally she was owned by the Strathcona Packing Company but very quickly went to Kingcome Navigation where, in 1938, her engine was replaced by a 600-horsepower Union diesel engine, a very powerful engine for that time. The *Ivanhoe*'s skipper for her first ten years at Kingcome was Arthur Stolberg. He was the master when she towed up Powell River's first paper-making machines. She moved logging camps for the Powell River Company, towed flat booms and Davis rafts, and served as its company yacht. This last function probably accounts for her reputation as one of the smartest-looking boats on the coast.

For fifty-seven years the *Ivanhoe* was a money-making boat in the Kingcome fleet and illustrates a point made by many old-time towboaters. One of the arguments advanced to justify crew reductions and the maintenance of boats by shore crews is that a seven-man boat—like the *Ivanhoe*—is no longer profitable to operate. Others dispute that assertion. They say that on such a boat, the low cost of maintenance—low since most of it was done by the boat's crew—offsets the higher wage costs. When Bill Dolmage managed Kingcome he was often pressed by the MacMillan Bloedel bureaucrats to get rid of the *Ivanhoe*; after all, it seemed odd for a sophisticated company to run such a relic. Dolmage always refused, pointing out that she was making money and her Union diesel was still running well after thirty-two years. That meant very little had to be spent on upkeep—and an engine overhaul at that time would have cost $30,000. A year after Dolmage retired in 1970, the *Ivanhoe* was sold to a boatbuilder on Galiano Island; he turned her into a houseboat and in 1980 put her up for sale for $190,000.

One of the finest log towers ever built was the *Sea Lion*, launched in 1905. She was built by Charles

Robertson for G.H. French, who was just getting started as Vancouver's first independent log tower. The wood for her timbers and planking was cut near Vancouver and taken to Saanich to dry over the winter, then brought to New Westminster to be cut at the Empire Sawmill. She was built in Vancouver at the site of the present Bayshore Hotel. The one-piece keel, cut from a choice 120-foot fir log, was 109 feet long, 2 feet wide and 3 feet deep. Overall she was 130 feet long with a 22-foot beam, and was powered by a triple-expansion steam engine imported from Scotland. She had a number of unusual features for a tug at that time: steam-powered steering gear and towing winch, a steel towline, dual steering and engine controls on the aft deck and, somewhat later, the first ship-to-shore radio and searchlight in B.C.

The *Sea Lion*'s first captain was Harry Young and her engineer was Lloyd Gore. After an ill-defined relationship with the British Canadian Lumber Company where Claude Thicke was in charge of her, the tug was chartered by Young and Gore who eventually purchased her in 1916. For six years they worked her themselves and made her the most elegant towboat on the coast. She was one of the tugs used to tow Davis rafts out of the Queen Charlottes during World War I and continued to tow rafts and booms until after World War II. Island Tug & Barge acquired the *Sea Lion* in 1952 when they took over Young and Gore. Shortly after that her boilers gave out, and the defunct *Active*'s 800-horsepower Enterprise diesel engine was installed in the *Sea Lion*. This conversion, plus modifications to the crew's quarters and a general refurbishing—including the installation of a compressed air system to operate her famous sliding-scale air whistle—cost $200,000. When Island Tug merged with the Vancouver Tug Boat Company in 1970, the Elworthys kept the *Sea Lion* and made her over into a yacht. Later, she was sold and put to work doing marine research, which she does to this day.

Shortly after Wallace built the *Ivanhoe*, his False Creek shipyard burned down and he set up a new yard near the foot of Lonsdale Avenue in North Vancouver. At this location, which eventually became Burrard Drydock, he continued to build tugs and became one of the earliest builders of steel tugs on the coast.

A former apprentice of Wallace's named Arthur Moscrop set up his own boatyard in False Creek, specializing in tugs. In 1914 he went to Prince Rupert to build the *Quinitsa* for Capt. H.B. Babington. She was a 58-foot boat with a 70-horsepower British Krumhout two-cylinder diesel engine, one of the first diesel tugs in the province. Eleven years later, renamed the *Island Planet*, she was used by Harold Elworthy to found Island Tug & Barge.

The many tugs built by Moscrop are central to the towboat industry of the next few decades. One of his early tugs was the *Swell*, a 70-foot steam tug that was used to found Victoria Tugboats. The *Projective*, the *R.F.M.*, the *Master* and the *Pronative* also came off his ways. When the Royal Canadian Mounted Police built their Arctic patrol boat the *St. Roch* at Burrard Drydock, he was hired to supervise her construction. Moscrop is considered the master builder of the wooden tug. Wood was the favoured material for tugs until after World War II, because it was cheap, of high quality and plentiful. Builders skilled in its use were available. Some steel tugs were built—the *Petrel* in 1907 and the *Point Grey* built by Wallace for the Canadian government in 1912—but in 1912 about twenty-five wooden tugs of more than 50 feet were launched.

Around the turn of the century, the basic design of the coastal log-towing boat was used to build a whole class of tugs of which people on the coast were only dimly aware. These tugs were operated mainly by the Canadian Pacific Railway on its lake and river service in the interior of the province. After the completion of the railway, farming, logging and mining had flourished in the Okanagan and the Kootenay valleys, but the mountain ranges that separated these interior valleys restricted the growth of highway transportation until well into this century. The initial development was therefore a combined railway-marine transportation system. The largest fleet with the biggest boats operated on Kootenay Lake. The *Ymir*, built at Nelson by J.W. Bulger in 1898, was a 77-foot propeller-driven steam tug. Bulger was probably also the builder of the *Valhalla* in 1901, the *Hosmer* in 1909 and the *Grant Hall* in 1918. The *Hosmer*, the largest, was nearly indistinguishable from a coastal log-towing boat; she was 109 feet long with a 21-foot beam and a deadweight of 104 tons. The chief occupation of these tugs

145. The CPR tug fleet on Kootenay Lake (*l. to r.*):
the *Ymir*, the *Valhalla* and the *Hosmer*,
sometime prior to 1925.

145

146

146. The CPR's *Grant Hall* tied up beside an empty
barge at Nelson on Kootenay Lake, 1937.

Arthur McLaren
President, Allied Shipbuilders

The reason for building the fairly big tugs early on was to tow in sailing ships. The early tugs didn't have towing winches. They were just a hold with a steam engine that could pull something that didn't have a steam engine.

The tugs were very much the same, a single-deck vessel with a deckhouse on it and a wheelhouse above that. They were all wooden construction, made from sawn frames rather than bent frames. They would get keel timbers that were ninety feet long by eighteen inches by eighteen inches—huge timbers. They had no trouble getting great long planks, which makes the whole boat better, because the fewer butt joints you have in the planking, the stronger the boat. The timber they had for them was beautiful stuff—some of them still have their original timbers.

A lot of the boatbuilders were Nova Scotians. During the 1860s and '70s, eastern Canada was a leading shipbuilding centre. These people came and saw the opportunity with the new land here, and realized that the only way you were going to get around was by water. It was quite obvious to them that there was going to be a demand for boats.

Most of the machinery was brought from Britain. The engines were dismantled after they were built so that they could be shipped, and were put together again here. The people who came out to put the machinery in nearly all came from Glasgow, because that's where they sold the engines in those days.

Most of these boats burned coal, not wood, because a tugboat isn't a very big vessel and it takes a hell of a lot of room to store wood. The first boats that burned oil in their boilers were the CPR and Union Steamship boats in about 1912 or '13. Some tugboats changed over to oil then; basically, it was just a question of changing the burners. Some boats never did get converted to burning oil; they just burned coal for the rest of their lives or until someone put a diesel engine in. There were one or two smaller boats with gasoline engines, but the danger of gasoline scared everybody, so that was never a success.

The next improvement that came along was the diesel, a slow-turning engine, nothing like what we have today. It gave twice the power, and while it was running you could still hear each other. They were very simple to run, didn't shake themselves to pieces and didn't drive you crazy with the noise.

After the war the high-speed diesel engine was developed, and that's where we are today. Once, a tugboat that was seventy or eighty feet long was 150 horsepower with a steam engine. When they turfed that out and got a 300-horsepower diesel they thought that was great. Then no one was happy unless they had 1,000 horsepower with a third conversion to a high-speed diesel.

Eventually the cost of metal construction came down and the cost of wooden construction went up. Manly built the first steel tugs in B.C. around 1944, little thirty-footers. But right at the end of the war they were bringing U.S. surplus tugs up here and rebuilding them, so there was no chance for new construction for quite a number of years. These surplus boats were eighty to eighty-five per cent wood because of the wartime steel shortage. And there were about half a dozen Canadian surplus tugs on the market, too. A lot of the surplus tugs had slow-speed diesels of 400 horsepower and carried a crew of nine. The owners said with 400 horsepower they couldn't put more than four men on it, otherwise it wouldn't make sense.

In the 1950s people got serious about the design of tugs. They found they could pack a hell of a lot more power into a small boat as engines got smaller, lighter and more powerful. Once a 200-horsepower diesel engine weighed fifteen tons; it only weighs a ton now. Then the owners found that you didn't need an engineer for a high-speed diesel, because you didn't have a huge complicated engine. That was the tin can phase: a steel hull with a big motor in it, and berths for four.

After the tin can phase, a certain amount of sanity settled over the industry. The Seafarers Union and the guild made demands for better accommodation. And the problem of noise, which had been neglected, was looked after. Then the whole question of stability came up, with the Coast Guard people demanding the boat be able to go over sixty degrees and come up again. These things are all good.

was to tow barges.

The same kind of towing work was done on the Arrow Lakes by three smaller tugs—the *Whatshan*, the *Columbia* and the *Smuggler*—which hauled bargeloads of lumber, ore and farm products. On Slocan Lake, the *Sandon* towed railcar barges. On Okanagan Lake, the *Castlegar* and the *Naramata*, a steel tug, towed barges. These two were joined much later, in 1926, by the *Pentowna*, a 127-foot diesel tug which had been built in Prince Rupert and shipped in pieces by rail. The *Pentowna* worked on the railcar barge run between Kelowna and Penticton.

A question often raised regarding these old wooden tugs, such as the *Sea Lion*, is why they survived seventy or eighty years of hard work while hundreds of boats built since have disappeared. The answer probably lies in the quality of their construction: a combination of the finest materials and excellent workmanship produced a number of vessels with built-in durability. In addition, some of these boats evoked a sense of pride among their owners and crews that was expressed in a meticulous approach to maintenance and operation. They were so well built and so well cared for that they survived the rigours of time and the conversions to changing needs. Unfortunately, the time has passed for most of these boats. They are no longer wanted as towboats: their power-to-size ratio is inadequate and their crew costs are too high. Their maintenance costs,

147

147. The CPR's *Naramata* circa 1920. She was a steel tug built in 1914 and carried a crew of ten. She towed barges between Penticton and Okanagan Landing.

148. The *La Pointe* undergoing conversion and re-engining to a 1,200-b.h.p. Fairbanks-Morse, 1953. About 1933 bought as the *Kingsway* by Harold Jones for Vancouver Tug and run as a steam tug until 1938 when she got an 805-b.h.p. Fairbanks-Morse diesel.

though not exorbitant given their size, make most of them too expensive for recreational or casual use. A few survive as yachts and houseboats, most of them owned by members of the Retired Tugboat Association. Some boats help to pay for themselves by doing odd jobs such as marine research. Only one steam tug, the *Master*, has survived with her engines still intact and functional; she is owned by the World Ship Society and has a berth at the Vancouver Maritime Museum.

The first major use of steel tugs in B.C. came about with the importation of a number of North Sea steam-powered fishing trawlers. These were heavy-duty oceangoing ships, built to withstand conditions in the North Atlantic. The first and largest of them, the *Kingsway* (later the *La Pointe*), was brought over by the Canadian Fishing Company. The next three came in 1912—the *Triumph*, the *Canada* and the *Imbricaria;* each was about 100 feet long and 150 tons, built in Yorkshire in the early 1890s. Canadian Fishing then brought over the *Andrew Kelly,* the *G.E. Foster* and the *James Carruthers,* all slightly larger at 118 feet and 230 tons. The problem with these trawlers was that there was no very profitable fishery for which they were suited; before long, they were tied up and out of use. Then, except for the *Triumph,* they were all converted into tugs.

Harold Hunter of White Rock Tug came across the *Foster,* the *Kelly* and the *Carruthers* tied up in Prince Rupert; White Rock bought the *Carruthers* and converted her into a towboat. Then Bill Dolmage bought her in 1933 and used her for log towing until 1940, when he sold her to the Gibson brothers. They used her for towing rafts and log barges until 1948, when they equipped her with a harpoon and sent her out whaling for the Western Whaling Corporation, of which the Gibsons were part owners. Soon after this venture, the *Carruthers* was gutted and her hull used as a herring scow. She sank with a full load of herring in Hecate Strait. Of the rest of the trawlers, the *Canada* sank in Puget Sound after colliding with an Alaska liner, and the *Foster* was scrapped in 1958 after serving Island Tug & Barge as the *Island Warrior.* Island Tug also bought the *Kelly* in 1941, renamed her the *Island Commander* and chartered her to the U.S. government in the Aleutians during the war. Seaspan got the *Island Commander* when it acquired Island Tug & Barge and,

considering the tug obsolete, sold her to Ken Higgs.

Starting in 1913, a number of innovative engines were tried out. Gasoline engines were available but were not popular because of the danger of explosions. Distillate engines, which ran on a sort of low-grade gasoline and even kerosene, were tried briefly. Semi-diesel engines were the type that gradually came into common use. They were big, slow-turning engines with a speed of 200 to 250 rpm, and were connected directly to the shaft so that it turned at the same speed. In order for the boat to go in reverse, engines often had to be stopped, then made to run backwards. They were tricky to operate and noisy compared to steam engines but they had a number of advantages. They were smaller for their power, started in only a few minutes, used a fuel that was easy to handle, and did not require the services of as many crew members. Most of the semi-diesels put in B.C. tugs came from American manufacturers—the Washington engine from Seattle, the Union from San Francisco and the Atlas from Oakland. A few, like the Dutch-made Stigert-Wayland that Claude Thicke put in the *VN & T No. 1* and the Swedish-built Advance in the *PRT No. 1*, were imported from Europe. Several makes of gasoline engines were built in Vancouver, most of them by Vivian or Easthope, but they were chiefly used in fish boats and yachts.

During the 1920s most of the 75- to 100-foot coastal log-towing boats built in the previous twenty-five years were converted from steam to semi-diesel engines. The availability of the semi-diesel engine also helped to bring about a boom in tug building. Many of these new tugs were smaller than the coastal log-towing boats, in the 35- to 55-foot range. By modern standards they were not very powerful but their pulling power was equal to that of many of the larger tugs of the steam era, and they had the advantage of requiring fewer crew members. Bill Dolmage's *Wee Giant* was an example of the type of boat to come. Built in 1925, she was 32 feet long, had a 36-horsepower, three-cylinder Gardiner semi-diesel engine, and was capable of towing a scow in open waters with a crew of one or two. Another such tug was Gulf of Georgia Towing's *Gabriola,* a 48-foot harbour tug with a 90-horsepower Washington-Estep diesel. Also typical of the period were Pacific Coyle's *Coyle No. 1,* a 56-foot tug with a

150-horsepower Washington-Estep diesel built by Moscrop, and Vancouver Tug's *La Reine*, a 75-foot tug with a 275-b.h.p., five-cylinder Washington-Estep diesel.

In 1929 a semi-diesel tug called the *Mikimiki* came off the ways in Seattle. She would change the face of towboating along the whole Pacific coast. Built for Young Brothers Towing of Honolulu, she was equipped with twin Fairbanks-Morse diesels that developed 1,120 horsepower, making her the most powerful diesel tug in the world. The *Mikimiki* was 125 feet long, 28 feet wide and drew 16 feet of water. On her maiden voyage to Hawaii she towed a 140-foot steel barge and shattered every towing record in the book. She was such

a successful boat that her design was later used for the World War II fleet of deep-sea tugs built by the U.S. government.

During the late 1930s and early 1940s high-speed diesel engines came on the market. These were even more compact than semi-diesels and allowed much more power to be put into a smaller boat. Because of the Depression and then restrictions on wartime boat-building, they did not play a significant role in towboats until after the war, with one notable exception. In 1939, Cosulich and Burt Towing built the *Red Fir No. 1*. Designed by George Peebles for towing on the Fraser River, she was 35 feet long, 12 feet wide and drew only 3 feet of water. The tug's semi-planing

149

149. The *Red Fir No. 2* (River Towing) loaded on a boat trailer at Hope, leaving for a salvage job on the Columbia River above Revelstoke. The photograph shows the shallowness of her draft.

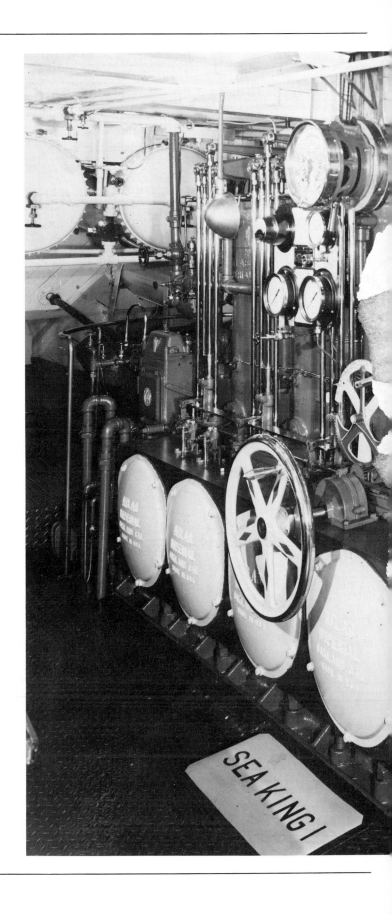

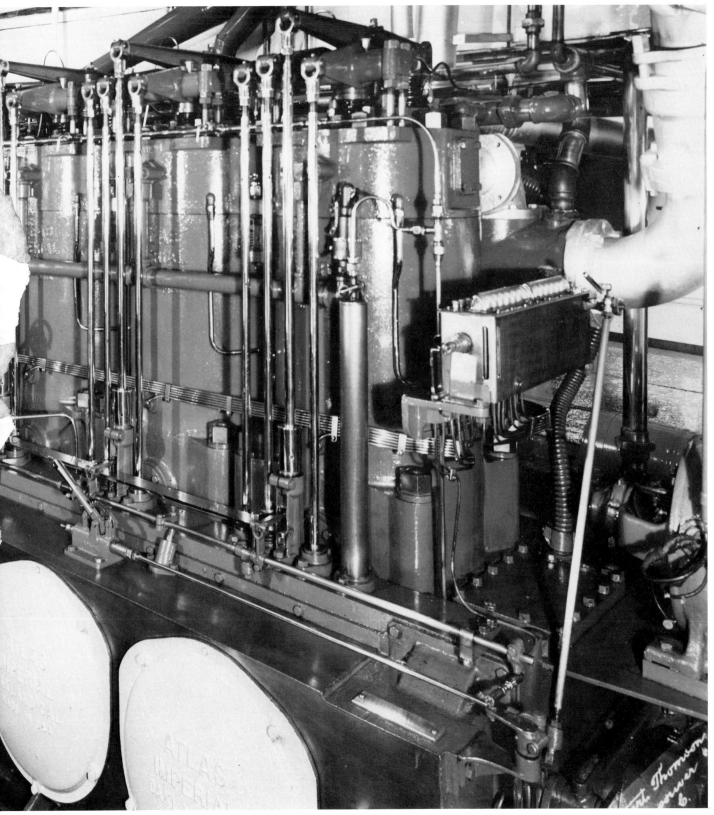

150. The engine of Dolmage Towing's *Sea King I* (ex-*Olive M*), a 400-horsepower Atlas diesel, circa 1940.

wooden hull had a channel towards the stern; the propeller was located in the recess to give the boat better clearance in the shallow river waters. This was not a radical departure in hull design, since it had been used on the small lake tugs in service near the coast and in other river tugs. However, a recessed propeller in combination with a powerful high-speed diesel and a shallow-draft hull created a specialized boat that was to be very successful on the river.

The two most popular high-speed diesel engines were the 165-horsepower General Motors and the 180-horsepower Cummins. The *Red Fir No. 1* was the first tug in B.C. to use the 165 GM; it replaced her original Vivian diesel engine. With that amount of

power in such a small, shallow-draft boat, she was able to run quickly up the river—at nine to ten knots— manoeuvre relatively large booms and run easily over sandbars and shallows that earlier boats of equal power were unable to go near.

The Cosulich brothers used the *Red Fir No. 1* as a prototype for a series of river boats, all with the same name but consecutively numbered. When their company River Towing became involved in the Silver Skagit logging operation in 1946, they built three more *Red Fir*s. These boats were not quite as beamy and were a little longer, giving them a bit more speed, and they were all equipped with 180 Cummins engines. Eventually there were a dozen such tugs, plus many similar

151. The *Sea Giant* (Dolmage Towing) was built in 1943. The 90-foot tug had a 6?5-b.h.p. Cooper-Bessemer engine and carried a crew of seven. When Vancouver Tug bought Dolmage Towing in 1956, she was renamed the *La Brise*.

river boats built by other companies and individuals.

After the war, the wooden tugs built by the U.S. government became surplus and were placed on sale. They had been constructed to meet exacting specifications and represented the last great flourish of wooden tug building on the Pacific coast. Most of them were equipped with heavy-duty diesel engines and could be purchased for a fraction of their worth. Bill Dolmage bought the *Sea Giant*, 98 feet with a 675-horsepower engine, for $43,000. In comparison, when Kingcome Navigation built its first large steel tug in 1952, the *Kingcome*—100 feet with a 700-horsepower Union diesel—she cost $475,000. The influx of these surplus tugs, between twenty-five and thirty of them including five or six of the *Mikimiki* class, re-equipped the B.C. towing industry. Since many of them were deep-sea boats, a number of companies, particularly Island Tug & Barge, developed the capability to tow in the open ocean which they had not had before. One of Island Tug's purchases was the *Sudbury*, later one of the most famous salvage tugs in the North Pacific.

In 1952, Pioneer Towing built the first fibreglass-covered tug in B.C., the *River Force*. She had lightweight, solid mahogany planks and frames and was powered by a 165 GM engine. She, too, was built for herding booms down the river, but her most remarkable feature was her speed: 18 knots. She astounded observers at the Seattle towboat races when she left

152

152. Vancouver Tug's *La Garde* being repowered with an 800-b.h.p. Cooper-Bessemer, in the 1950s. Built in 1942 and powered with a 300-horsepower Washington out of the *La Reine*, she was designed for a 600-horsepower engine (not available until after the war).

153. Close-up of Kort nozzle of the *Pacific Force*
(Pacific Towing Services), built in 1980.

154. Close-up of the towing winch of the *Gulf Mariner*, circa 1950.

every other boat in her class far behind.

The importation of war surplus tugs discouraged the building of new boats but there was a lot of work involved in refittings, repairs and conversions of both older and surplus tugs. The construction of new tugs did not become a major concern until the mid-1950s. By then the advances in boatbuilding techniques since the last great tug-building boom in the 1920s were enormous. The wartime shipbuilding programs had advanced the art of steel construction from the slow, expensive riveted plates to welded seams, and heavy-duty diesels had been replaced by high-speed diesels. A vast array of new equipment was available; it was expensive but would greatly improve performance and safety. This included electronic navigation aids such as radar, automatic pilots and depth sounders; sophisticated communications systems; improved propulsion devices such as the Kort nozzle to increase propeller thrust, and variable-pitch propellers; towline safety-release hooks and tensioning mechanisms to maintain an even strain on towlines; antivibration materials to dampen the effects of high-speed diesel engines. A number of shipyards—John Manly, Benson, Mercer, Burrard Drydock, B.C. Marine, Allied, Matsumoto, Star and Yarrows—were ready and well equipped to start building a new kind of towboat.

A number of factors affected the design and construction of these boats. Price was a major considera-

155

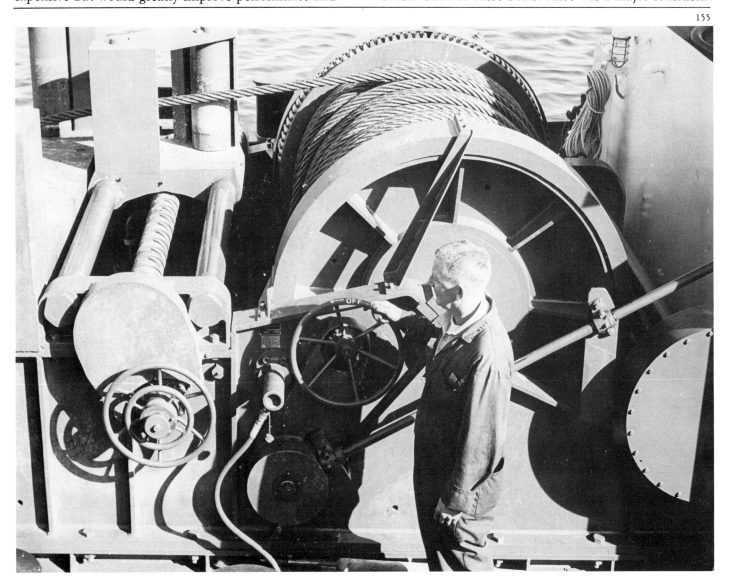

155. Close-up of the towing winch of Island Tug's *Island Champion*. The reel has a capacity of 2,400 feet of 1¾-inch cable, and is equipped with two links to permit towage of three barges simultaneously. The 91-foot tug was an American war surplus boat.

Terry Waghorn
President, C.H. Cates & Sons

When I was working on the boats myself I took a keen interest in them and could see their weaknesses and strengths. I'm talking about the original design of the wooden tug.

When I had the opportunity to build my first tug, I went to Robert Allan, the naval architect, because in my opinion he was probably the best around. He was green as grass as far as ship-handling tugs in Vancouver harbour was concerned, because nobody except Cates was doing it.

I got him over here and we went out on several different jobs, and I showed him: this is great, this isn't very efficient, this is no good, what can we do about this, this is what I want, etc. So we built the *Charles H. Cates XX*. It was the first steel tug that the company had and performed just great, but it had its weaknesses. So we built another and correctd those weaknesses, and then another one. Every time we built a tug we changed it, until now we're only into cosmetic changes.

The first thing I went to was twin screws, for manoeuvrability. At that time the Kort nozzles had come out, which was a great thing. You're looking at twenty-five to thirty per cent more thrust with a nozzle, so we went into that. Then we went into a shallower draft tug, more beamy, so it could slide, could go sideways without heeling over. We also got into rudder power. We had only two rudders on the first twin screw. The next time we put four rudders on. The first one, we had a skeg on it; the next one we took the skeg off.

We had no external keel on the next one. There was no drag, so these hulls are pretty smooth all the way around. Nothing in front of the propeller, no obstruction of any kind.

Fendering is very important in our work. Every time we go out on a job, we collide. Those aircraft tires we tried were a big improvement.

Then we were into noise abatement on the tugs. We always wanted our tugs quiet, because it's more pleasant to have a quieter tug and our communications are important. Long before the regulations came, we were striving for quiet tugs. We've got some pretty sophisticated materials and technology now. We've isolated the wheelhouse from the hull, engine from the engine bed, the exhaust system from the rest of the tug. Lead is being used in different components to make these tugs quieter.

Years ago when they built sailing ships every boat was that shape. We don't need to have boats that shape any more, for our work. Now we've got a great blunt bow on our new tugs. The last one I built was a great big full-nosed thing. We designed it so that we can pivot much better against the side of the ship we're assisting.

In the latest tugs, we've gone into a new towing system with a release hook—an abort system—which is much safer. You're not going to get flipped over if you're hooked on the stern of a ship when he goes ahead, get broadside to him or caught in his wash. All the skipper has to do is press a button and he's long gone.

These are some of the improvements that have been made. The towing industry has come a long way.

tion, for a 100-foot tug cost close to half a million dollars. Owners wanted more powerful engines and fewer crew members in order to cut back on the escalating labour costs of operation. The shipbuilding subsidy designed to increase employment in the shipyards provided an incentive, but it was not always conducive to the building of great boats. One simplified approach to this situation, as mentioned earlier, was the development of a tug that had a powerful motor in a steel hull. Fortunately, a more common approach was to combine the new technology with the designs of B.C.'s naval architects. By the early 1960s a flood of new tugs was appearing, some built with the quality that could evoke the kind of pride and

attention that had developed during the 1920s. The *Kingcome* was such a tug, as was the *Lorne Yorke*, built for F.M. Yorke & Son in 1960. She was a 94-foot steel tug with twin 400-horsepower Caterpillar diesels, designed by Robert Allan and built at Allied. She was named after the *Lorne* by Greg Yorke, who had fallen in love with the old steam tug as a child, and was put to work towing railcar barges. The *Ocean Master,* also designed by Allan, was built in Holland for Great West Towing & Salvage. She was a 126-foot deep-sea tug with 1,800-horsepower Stork-Werkspoor diesels. Allan also designed the *Harold A. Jones,* a 136-foot tug powered by two 1,750-b.h.p. Stork-Werkspoor diesels, for Vancouver Tug. Island Tug & Barge had the *Island*

156

156. Vancouver Tug's *Harold A. Jones*, the flagship of their fleet, with five empty chip barges in tow, coming into Vancouver harbour circa 1970. The tug was built by Star Shipyards and named for the firm's founder.

157. Pacific Towing Service's *Pacific Force* on the
ways, 1980. The semicircular tubing on the
prow is shaped to hold tire fenders.

158. Top view of the *Pacific Force*, showing the angular, raked-back twin smokestacks.

159. In 1950, the wheelhouse of the *Gulf Mariner*.

160. In 1980, the wheelhouse of the *Pacific Force*.

Mariner built in England. She was a 97-foot twin-screw tug with two 660-horsepower Lister-Blackstone diesels. On her way to B.C. she took in tow the hull of another 100-foot tug built in Quebec.

This building program continued on into the 1970s with dozens of new tugs coming off the ways. C.H. Cates & Sons and Westminster Tug began refining their designs, building some of the most advanced ship-berthing tugs in the world. For Cates, Allan designed tugs with blunter bows and twin propellers for better manoeuvrability in pushing, and with shallower drafts and wider hulls so they could move sideways without rolling. The superstructures were set well back and sloped in so that the tugs could get in close under the hulls of the ships they were assisting.

During the same period there was a great increase in the construction of steel barges, largely for specialized uses. In 1962, Island Tug built two of the largest flat-deck oceangoing barges in the world, the *Island Exporter* and the *Island Importer*. They were 360 feet long, 75 feet wide and had a capacity of 10,800 tons. These barges were designed by Robert Allan and built by Yarrows to carry crushed limerock from Texada Island to Portland, Oregon. In the early 1960s, Vancouver Tug ordered, in a single contract, twenty-five steel barges from Yarrows. Dozens of log barges were also built during this time, culminating in the self-loading, self-propelled, self-dumping *Haida Monarch* and *Haida Brave*, designed by Gerry Talbot for Kingcome Navigation.

The list of tugs constructed then is very long. In 1964 a survey determined that about fifty new tugs or repowering of older tugs were underway, at a cost of about $30 million, on behalf of Pacific northwest towing companies. Well over half of these involved B.C. companies. It was a tremendous revival of the art of towboat building, beginning in the 1960s and tapering off a bit in the 1970s.

Naturally, not all of these vessels will be great tugs, but a few are certain to endure, be refitted and transformed, and slowly become classics in the mould of the *Sea Lion*, the *Lorne* and the *Ivanhoe*. The few wooden tugs still working will gradually go out of service and find berths as yachts. And the tin can tugs will disappear into the scrap yards where they belong.

To a large degree, the fate of these tugs, along with the companies who own them and the industry as a whole, depends on factors beyond their control, for towboating is an industry which exists to fill the water transportation needs of other industries. However, as the history of tugboats and the industry has shown, the people in the industry have always been eager to improve the design of their boats and to invent or adopt new towing techniques to meet changing demands. This pioneering attitude, combined with a willingness to make heavy investments in innovative technology, promises that towboats will continue to improve and evolve in surprising directions. The legends of the future are being built today.

161. The old and the new: the *Master* and the *Haida Transporter* tied up at the same dock. The *Master* is the oldest surviving steam tug on the coast. The *Haida Transporter* (Kingcome Navigation) is a self-propelled railcar carrier with a capacity of twenty-six cars.

Acknowledgements

The extract from the 10 August 1832 letter written by George Simpson, in the Hudson's Bay Company Archives, D.4/99 folio 16d and D.4/99 folio 17, is printed by permission of the Hudson's Bay Company.

The extract from the 17 May 1836 entry in the log of the *Beaver* is printed by permission of the Provincial Archives of British Columbia.

The passages from *Tidal Actions in British Columbia Waters* (privately published) and the extract from the text of a speech, both by Capt. Charles Warren Cates, are reprinted by kind permission of his wife and daughters.

The aural history transcripts of the author's interviews with Ray Bicknell, Jim Byrn, Bill Dolmage, Drydie Jones, Arthur McLaren, O.H. New, Alex Rodgers, Bill Sankey, Lloyd Sias, Doug Stone, Ed Taylor and Terry Waghorn are printed by permission of the individuals involved.

The aural history transcripts of interviews with Capt. Mickey Balatti are printed by permission of the Sound and Moving Images Division, Provincial Archives of British Columbia.

The aural history transcripts of the author's interviews with Claude Thicke are printed by kind permission of his wife.

The extract from the article by Capt. Don Peck which appeared in the 1 July 1972 issue of the Victoria *Daily Colonist Islander* magazine is reprinted by kind permission of Mrs. D.W. Peck.

The profile plan (1925) of the tugboat on the front endpapers (probably the *St. Faith*) is printed by permission of the Vancouver Maritime Museum.

The profile plan (1975) of the 140-foot, 5,750-b.h.p. oceangoing tugboat on the back endpapers is printed by permission of Seaspan International Ltd.

Frontispiece photograph © Toby Rankin/Masterfile

The photographs (referred to by number) are printed by permission of the following:

W.T.G. Atwood: 151

Campbell River & District Museum: 31

Council of Marine Carriers: 20, 39, 40, 46, 59, 65, 69, 70, 73, 85, 102, 107, 109, 114, 134, 139, 140, 147

Capt. W.G. Dolmage: 77, 103, 150, 161

Gordon Gibson: 71

Evan D. Jones: 4, 47

Capt. Robert D. MacDonald: 89, 91, 95

Maritime Museum of British Columbia: 13, 27, 54, 86

Pacific Towing Services Ltd.: 122, 133, 153, 157, 158, 160

Provincial Archives of British Columbia: 10, 48, 56, 145, 146

RivTow Straits Ltd.: 1, 2, 75, 83, 93, 106, 108, 116, 117, 119, 125, 131, 132, 135, 149

Seaspan International Ltd.: 3, 88, 92, 94, 96, 97, 101, 110, 111, 112, 115, 120, 121, 130, 148, 152, 155, 156

Capt. Lloyd Sias: 66

Douglas E. Stone: 60, 64, 80

Alf and Helen Talbot: 138

Vancouver City Archives: 8, 9, 12, 14, 15, 16, 21, 22, 25, 26, 28, 34, 49, 50, 61, 99

Vancouver Maritime Museum: 6, 7, 11, 19, 23, 30, 35, 38, 41, 42, 43, 44, 45, 52, 53, 55, 57, 58, 62, 67, 68, 72, 76, 78, 79, 81, 82, 84, 87, 90, 98, 100, 104, 105, 123, 124, 126, 127, 128, 129, 136

Vancouver Public Library: 5, 17, 18, 24, 29, 32, 33, 36, 37, 51, 63, 74

Al Zueff: 113, 141, 143, 144

Index

References to photograph captions, by number, are in italic type.